# Daniel

MEN *of*
CHARACTER

# Daniel
## Standing Firm
## for God

# GENE A. GETZ
Foreword by John F. Walvoord

PUBLISHING GROUP

Nashville, Tennessee

© 1998
by Gene A. Getz
All rights reserved
Printed in the United States of America
978-0-8054-6172-5
Published by B&H Publishing Group, Nashville, Tennessee
Dewey Decimal Classification: 224.5
Subject Heading: DANIEL (BIBLICAL CHARACTER, BIBLE.
\ O. T.—BIOGRAPHY)
Library of Congress Card Catalog Number: 97-49918
Unless otherwise noted, Scripture quotations are from the Holy Bible,
New International Version, copyright © 1973, 1978, 1984 by
International Bible Society. Other versions cited are NASB, the
New American Standard Bible, © the Lockman Foundation,
1960, 1962, 1963, 1968, 1971, 1973, 1975, 1977; used by
permission; and KJV, the King James Version.

Italicized words in Scripture quotations indicate the author's
emphasis.

**Library of Congress Cataloging-in-Publication Data**

Getz, Gene A.
      Daniel : standing firm for God / Gene A. Getz
         p. cm. - (Men of character)
      Includes bibliographical references.
      ISBN 0-8054-6172-8 (pbk.)
         1. Daniel (Biblical character). 2. Bible. O. T.—Biography
I. Title.    II. Series: Getz, Gene A.  Men of character.
      BS580.D2G47   1998
      224'.5092—dc21                                    97-49918
                                                            CIP

12 13 14 15  •  16 15 14 13 12

*I*t's a unique privilege to dedicate this "Men of Character" study on Daniel's life to Dr. John F. Walvoord. Currently chancellor of Dallas Theological Seminary, he served as its second president from 1952–1986 and was on the Dallas faculty for fifty years.

There are several reasons I have chosen to dedicate this study to this man. First, he has distinguished himself over the years as an astute and dedicated theologian, specializing in the area of eschatology. His contributions to helping all of us understand the prophetic sections of Scripture have been enormous.

The second reason for this dedication is that Dr. Walvoord has served God faithfully for a lifetime. As I pen these words, he is approximately the same age as Daniel as he completed his faithful service in Babylon. Just so, Dr. Walvoord's commitment to living a noncompromising life has been evident to all of us who have worked closely with him.

My third reason is more personal. Dr. Walvoord, along with Dr. Howard Hendricks, invited me to join the distinguished faculty at Dallas Theological Seminary. This decision affected my life and ministry career dramatically. The encouragement he gave me as a professor challenged me to explore the Scriptures with my students, particularly in the area of ecclesiology, which also launched me into an extensive church-planting ministry. This experience also challenged me to expand extensively my written ministry.

Thanks, dear brother in Christ. You've marked my life. From a human point of view, without your encouragement, I would not have penned the "Men of Character" series, including this book on Daniel's life.

# Contents

# Foreword

*T*o Daniel the prophet was given the tremendous task of recording God's prophetic revelation concerning the prophetic program for Israel as well as the prophetic program for the nations of the world. No other prophet in the Old or New Testaments provides the comprehensive picture that these prophecies provide.

While the Book of Daniel is basically a prophetic book because of its contents, many chapters of the book deal with Daniel's experiences as well as those of Nebuchadnezzar, all pointing to very practical conclusions related to the Christian life and testimony. Daniel is one of the few principal characters of the Old Testament concerning whom there is not a word of criticism. Daniel himself was an amazing individual. While still a teenager he had to stand before Nebuchadnezzar and describe the meaning of the king's dream. His statement was an outstanding demonstration of Daniel's gifts and his capacity to speak to the king in a Babylonian language which he had learned only a few years before. It was an outstanding illustration of giving God the glory for what amounted to tremendous divine revelation.

It is significant that the Book of Daniel devotes a whole chapter to the issue of Daniel and his companions observing the Jewish laws regarding food. While to many this may seem incidental, it is obvious that the Book of Daniel would never have been written if Daniel had given in to the standards of the Babylonian religion and had abandoned his Jewish heritage.

Even in his final hours as a man over eighty years of age, Daniel stands tall, capable, and completely yielded to God. While many Christians may not know much about the Book of Daniel, many have heard of "Daniel in the lions' den" with that story's challenge of complete obedience to the revealed will of God.

This exposition of the Book of Daniel, more so than any commentary which I have read, is distinguished by its practical application and the reduction of difficult doctrines to explanations that anyone can understand. The challenge to us to be completely obedient to God in the most difficult circumstances is the outstanding message of this book.

*Dr. John F. Walvoord*

# Daniel: Serving God for a Lifetime

*T*his book is primarily a study in character, and Daniel is a remarkable man who stands tall on the pages of the Old Testament. His experiences and exploits in Babylon emblazon the Jewish hall of faith with illuminating portraits that are inspiring examples for us all. Unlike many of his great forefathers—even Old Testament giants like Abraham, Moses, Jacob, and David—Daniel consistently and faithfully served God for a lifetime! He is definitely in the same league with men like Joseph, Joshua, Nehemiah, and Samuel. Even on this kind of "dream team," he would definitely be appointed captain.

Though Daniel was naturally endowed with a good mind and a strong body, he must have also had a strong spiritual foundation. Though we know nothing of his parents, someone must have diligently taught him his Jewish heritage and God's divine plans for the children of Israel. Even as a teenager who had been forcibly removed from his home and exposed to all of the evil influences in a deceitful and pagan environment that was permeated with immoral and occult practices, Daniel demonstrated unusual wisdom and discretion in applying what he knew about God's laws. He also lived an extremely disciplined life, whether diligently applying himself as a student or in carrying out the tasks assigned to him.

Needless to say, from a human perspective, Daniel was an exceptional young man. However, he was also uniquely blessed with supernatural gifts for understanding, interpreting, and receiving direct messages from God. But in spite of his divine attributes, Daniel lived most of his life like all of us. His days were filled with demanding responsibilities and difficult tasks—some challenging and some boring—that called for a lot of gut-level determination and perseverance.

Though there are large time gaps in Daniel's life story, we have enough biblical information to conclude that he lived a very consistent life, never veering from the path God had marked out for him. We first meet him as a young teenager—around fifteen years old—and leave him in his mid-eighties.

The first six chapters of the book that bears his name focus primarily on Daniel's personal experiences as a servant-leader (the historical section), and the second six chapters focus on his visions and dreams (the prophetic section). The events and Daniel's approximate age when they transpired can be outlined and described as follows:

## Historical Section (Chapters 1–6)

| Chapters | Events | Daniel's Age |
|---|---|---|
| 1 | Taken into Babylonian captivity | 15 |
| 2 | Interpreting Nebuchadnezzar's first dream (the huge image) | 17 |
| 3 | Daniel's three friends cast into the fiery furnace | 19 or 20 |
| 4 | Interpreting Nebuchadnezzar's second dream regarding the huge tree | 45–50 |
| 5 | Interpreting the handwriting on the wall at Belshazzar's feast | early 80s |
| 6 | Delivered from the den of lions | c. 83 |

## Prophetic Section (Chapters 7–12)

| | | |
|---|---|---|
| 7–8 | Daniel's visions and dreams | mid-60s |
| 9 | Daniel's seventy "sevens" prophecy | early 80s |
| 10–12 | Final dreams and visions | mid-80s |

All of the historical events recorded by Daniel in chapters 1–6 happened chronologically. However, the visions and dreams recorded in the prophetic section (chapters 7–12) overlap the events in the historical section beginning when Daniel was in his mid-sixties. This can be illustrated more clearly in the following graphic:

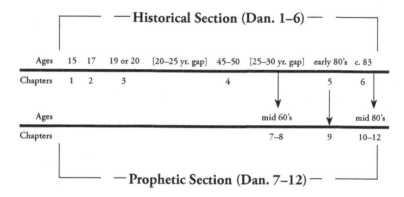

This overview indicates that Daniel's life was not always characterized by visions and dreams and other direct messages from the Lord. There were great time periods in his life—nearly fifty years—that were probably quite mundane and filled with experiences that called for the same routine disciplines and skills a great majority of us need to practice every day. Perhaps these time periods in his life yield the most challenging lessons for us today. Daniel was indeed "prepared" to live for God "in season and out of season" (2 Tim. 4:2).

As with all Old Testament personalities, we can learn a great deal from Daniel. Principles that flow from his life and his close associates are powerful and enduring. Daniel faced and lived his life as a great inspiration and model. His ability not only to survive but to win respect and prosper make the principles that emerge from his experience even more potent and practical.

Welcome to an exciting study! Though there are various opinions regarding dates, names, events, and what actually happened in certain instances, I've chosen certain theories and interpretations that I personally feel can be supported by the natural flow of the biblical text. This approach forms the basis for some of my speculative questions and possible conclusions. I trust this study will motivate you to dig deeper into more sophisticated commentaries written on the book of Daniel. Hopefully, most of what you read will support my own overall conclusions.

I've also built this study on a very important assumption that characterizes all conservative students of Scripture: Daniel recorded his visions and dreams during his lifetime and before these events actually happened. This leads to an even more fundamental assumption. Daniel was a true prophet who "spoke from God as" he was "carried along by the Holy Spirit" (2 Pet. 1:21).

*Dr. Gene A. Getz*

## Chapter 1

# *Reaping What We Sow*
### Read Daniel 1:1–12

*H*ave you ever met a man who virtually "spit" in the face of God? If you haven't, you're about to meet one. If he were Adolf Hitler or Joseph Stalin, we might not be so surprised and shocked. However, this man was a king over God's people. His name was Jehoiakim, and his behavior was despicable, arrogant, flippant, and totally irresponsible. He had no regard whatsoever for the God of Abraham, Isaac, and Jacob. Like all people who violate God's will on a consistent basis, Jehoiakim eventually reaped what he had sown.

It happened in the third year of his reign. We read that "the Lord delivered Jehoiakim king of Judah into" the hand of Nebuchadnezzar, the king of Babylon (Dan. 1:2). At the same time, Nebuchadnezzar took some of Judah's choice young men back to Babylon to be trained and equipped to serve in his court. But we're getting ahead of the story. To understand **why** all of this happened, we need to understand, at least in brief, the history of the children of Israel.

## *Prime Real Estate, a Horde of People, and a Promised Savior!*

Israel's story actually began about 1,600 years earlier when God called Abraham out of the pagan city of Ur, a large commercial center in the Mesopotamian valley. Everyone in the whole world had turned away from the one true God—including Abraham and his family. World conditions had been just as wicked in the days of Noah. At that time Noah and his family were the only God-fearing people on earth (Gen. 6:9). This was not true of Abraham and his family. They were idolaters.

## Three Powerful Promises

God in His sovereign grace began to unfold His redemptive plan to save mankind from eternal destruction when He revealed Himself to Abraham and made him three promises. First, He was going to bless Abraham with a permanent home—the land of Canaan. Second, God also promised Abraham a heritage—a great nation of people. Most importantly, God promised that all people everywhere would be blessed through his offspring (Gen. 12:1–3). With this final promise, God was referring to a future "son of Abraham," God's eternal Son, Jesus Christ, who would be born in due time and become the Savior of the world (Gal. 3:6–9).

## Twelve Sons (Israel)

Abraham responded to God's call and His command to leave Ur. By faith, he entered the land of Canaan. Eventually, he had two sons, Ishmael and Isaac (Gen. 16:15; 21:3). According to God's sovereign plan, Isaac became the chosen heir, and through him, God's three promises to Abraham continued to unfold (22:15–18).

Isaac also had two sons, Esau and Jacob (25:24–26). Again, according to God's divine decree, Jacob became the channel God used to continue to carry out His specific promises (28:10–15). In turn, Jacob had twelve sons, and since the Lord changed Jacob's name to Israel, these men were eventually called "the sons of Israel" (32:28).

## *The Egyptian Experience*

At this point in Old Testament history, the plot thickens. Jacob's older sons hated their younger brother, Joseph, because their father favored him. They conspired against this young man and sold him to a band of Midianites, who transported him to Egypt where he became a slave (37:28, 36). Though Joseph faced some incredible trials—including sexual harassment and an unwarranted imprisonment—he never allowed bitterness to capture his soul. God honored his sterling character and he soon became a very successful man. He was only thirty years old when the Pharaoh appointed him as his executive leader, giving him virtually unlimited authority to govern the whole country.

Eventually and ironically, God used Joseph to save his whole family from a devastating famine in the land of Canaan. In spite of his brothers' cruelty, Joseph arranged for his father, Jacob, and all his children and grandchildren to come to live in one of the most productive areas in Egypt.

For approximately 400 years, the children of Israel grew into a great nation, just as God had promised Abraham. However, long after the king of Egypt—who had favored Joseph—had died, a pharaoh came to power who was threatened by this rapidly growing group of people (Exod. 1:8). In order to discourage and demoralize them, he demanded more than these slaves could ever deliver.

But God did not forget His promises to Abraham, Isaac, and Jacob (Israel). In His divine timing, the Lord raised up Moses, one of the greatest prophets and leaders who ever lived (Deut. 34:10–12). Eventually Moses led the children of Israel out of Egypt and across the Red Sea. When they camped at Mount Sinai, God gave Israel the Ten Commandments and other laws to guide them in their religious and community life. However, because of their persistent disobedience, God disciplined them by making them wander in the wilderness for forty years. But again, true to His promises, the Lord eventually anointed Joshua as Moses' successor, who in turn led the children of Israel into Canaan.

## A Powerful Takeover

Joshua was a very faithful and successful leader in Israel. As a result of three dynamic campaigns, his army captured much of the land of Canaan—again as God had promised. However, before they took possession of all the land—when "Joshua was old and well advanced in years"—the Lord told him to stop doing battle and to divide the conquered land among the twelve tribes (Josh. 13:1).

As Joshua came to the end of his life, he issued a powerful challenge to the children of Israel:

> *Now fear the Lord and serve him with all faithfulness. Throw away the gods your forefathers worshiped beyond the River and in Egypt, and serve the Lord But if serving the Lord seems undesirable to you, then choose for yourselves this day whom you will serve, whether the gods your forefathers served beyond the River, or the gods of the Amorites, in whose land you are living. But as for me and my household, we will serve the Lord (24:14–15).*

> *At this point in their history, the children of Israel responded very positively—even enthusiastically—to Joshua's charge. "Far be it from us to forsake the Lord to serve other gods!" they cried out in one accord (24:16).*

## A Cycle of Degeneration and Regeneration

Initially, God's people kept their promise and "served the Lord throughout the lifetime of Joshua and of the elders who outlived him" (24:31). However, an incredible thing happened. After their godly leader died, and "after that whole generation had been gathered to their fathers, another generation grew up, who knew neither the Lord nor what he had done for Israel" (Judg. 2:10). Sadly, their ignorance led them to forsake the Lord and to begin to follow and worship "various gods of the peoples around them" (2:12). It took only one generation for degeneration to take place.

This national unbelief and indulgence in pagan practices introduced Israel to a terrible period of ups and downs known as the time of the Judges. Again and again, Israel "did evil in the sight of the Lord," experienced defeat from their enemies, and were taken into slavery. And again and again, they repented and cried out to the Lord—and each time, God mercifully raised up leaders to deliver them from their enemies.

## *Rejecting the King of Kings*

Eventually, God raised up a righteous judge named Samuel who did more to lead the children of Israel in the right direction than any other leader since Joshua. However, toward the end of Samuel's life, the children of Israel asked for a king. They wanted to be like the pagan people around them. With this request, they were actually rejecting the King of kings. Though the Lord was very offended, He charged Samuel to go ahead and give them what they wanted and to anoint a handsome young man named Saul to be king of Israel.

Though Saul made a good start, eventually pride and anger withered his soul. Consequently, God rejected him as king and instructed Samuel to anoint David instead. The Lord allowed Saul to continue to rule for a number of years; but, knowing that God had already anointed David to replace him, Saul tried often to thwart God's plan. Sadly, he ended his life by committing suicide.

At this point, David assumed the throne and for years provided the children of Israel with godly leadership. Tragically, after a very successful reign, this "man after God's heart" also failed miserably. He committed adultery with Bathsheba, fathered a child, and, in order to try to cover his sin, David issued an order to have her husband, Uriah, sent to the front lines in battle. As David had hoped, Uriah fell mortally wounded. David had compounded his immoral act by committing murder.

Because of these terrible sins, God told David that "the sword" would "never depart" from his house—and it never did (2 Sam. 12:10). Though the Lord mercifully forgave David because of his sincere repentance, he faced the horrible consequences the rest of his life. He too reaped what he had sown. When he died, his son Solomon became the king of Israel.

Solomon also made a great start. Rather than asking for riches and great success, he asked God for wisdom to lead Israel. Because of this unselfish and humble approach to his kingship, God gave Solomon what he had not asked for. In addition to making him one of the wisest men who ever lived, He also gave him great riches and enviable success. Even the queen of Sheba came to learn from Solomon and marveled at his material prosperity and kingly power.

## The Divided Kingdom

If we didn't know the end of the story, it would be difficult to predict Solomon's tragic ending. Because Solomon violated God's will by marrying foreign wives and participating in idolatry, the kingdom of Israel was divided. Jeroboam ruled the northern tribes and Rehoboam ruled the southern tribes (Judah and Benjamin). Both kingdoms continued to be characterized by flagrant idolatry and immorality. Though it is beyond comprehension, some of these people actually offered their own children as sacrifices to pagan gods.

As the Lord had forewarned, He judged all Israel for their terrible sins. The Assyrians took the northern tribes into captivity, and eventually, those in the southern kingdom were deported by the Babylonians.

## Arrogance Personified

This brief history brings us to the events described in the opening verses of the Book of Daniel. When Nebuchadnezzar attacked Jerusalem, Jehoiakim was king of Judah—the eighteenth king since Rehoboam (see fig. 1 for an historical perspective). Out of all of the kings of Judah, eleven were wicked men—and Jehoiakim was one of the worst. Like his

# LEADERS IN ISRAEL

| | | |
|---|---|---|
| | Moses | Exod. 3:7–10 |
| | Joshua | Josh. 1:1–9 |

**Judges**

| | | |
|---|---|---|
| 1. | Othniel | Judg. 3:9 |
| 2. | Ethud | Judg. 3:15 |
| 3. | Shamgar | Judg. 3:31 |
| 4. | Deborah | Judg. 4:5 |
| 5. | Gideon | Judg. 6:36 |
| 6. | Abimelech | Judg.9:1 |
| 7. | Tola | Judg. 10:1 |
| 8. | Jair | Judg. 10:3 |
| 9. | Jephthah | Judg. 11:11 |
| 10. | Ibzan | Judg. 12:8 |
| 11. | Elon | Judg. 12:11 |
| 12. | Abdon | Judg. 12:13 |
| 13. | Samson | Judg. 16:30 |
| 14. | Eli | 1 Sam. 4:18 |
| 15. | Samuel | 1 Sam. 7:15 |

**First Kings**

| | | |
|---|---|---|
| 1. | Saul | 1 Sam. 10:1 |
| 2. | David | 1 Sam. 16:13 |
| 3. | Solomon | 1 Kings 1:29–30 |

## Divided Kingdom

| Kings of Israel | | Kings of Judah | |
|---|---|---|---|
| 1. Jeroboam I | 1 Kings 11:28 | 1. Rehoboam | 1 Kings 11:43 |
| 2. Nabad | 1 Kings 14:20 | 2. Abijah, or Abijam | 1 Kings 14:31 |
| 3. Baasha | 1 Kings 15:16 | 3. Asa | 1 Kings 15:8 |
| 4. Elah | 1 Kings 16:8 | 4. Jehoshaphat | 1 Kings 15:24 |
| 5. Zimri | 1 Kings 16:15 | 5. Jehoram | 2 Chron. 21:1 |
| 6. Omri | 1 Kings 16:16 | 6. Ahaziah | 2 Kings 8:25 |
| 7. Ahab | 1 Kings 16:29 | 7. Athaliah (Queen) | 2 Kings 8:26 |
| 8. Ahaziah | 1 Kings 22:40 | 8. Joash, or Jehoash | 2 Kings 11:2 |
| 9. Jehoram, or Joram | 2 Kings 1:17 | 9. Amaziah | 2 Kings 14:1 |
| 10. Jehu | 1 Kings 19:16 | 10. Azariah, or Uzziah | 2 Kings 15:1 |
| 11. Jehoahaz | 2 Kings 10:35 | 11. Jotham | 2 Kings 15:5 |
| 12. Jehoash | 2 Kings 13:10 | 12. Ahaz | 2 Kings 15:38 |
| 13. Jeroboam II | 2 Kings 14:23 | 13. Hezekiah | 2 Kings 16:20 |
| 14. Zechariah | 2 Kings 14:29 | 14. Manasseh | 2 Kings 21:1 |
| 15. Shallum | 2 Kings 15:10 | 15. Amon | 2 Kings 21:19 |
| 16. Menahem | 2 Kings 15:14 | 16. Josiah | 2 Kings 13:2 |
| 17. Pekahiah | 2 Kings 15:23 | 17. Jehoahaz, or Shallum | 2 Kings 23:30 |
| 18. Pekah | 2 Kings 15:25 | **18. Jehoiakim** | **2 Kings 23:34** |
| 19. Hoshea | 2 Kings 15:30 | 19. Jehoiachin, or Jeconiah | 2 Kings 24:6 |
| | | 20. Zedekiah, or Mattaniah | 2 Kings 24:17 |

Assyrian Captivity (740–721 B.C.)

Babylonian Captivity (605–586 B.C.)

**Fig. 1 - Historical Perspective on Leadership in Israel**

predecessor, Jehoahaz, "he did evil in the eyes of the Lord" (2 Kings 23:32).

Jehoiakim committed one of his most flagrant sins when he not only ignored the word of the Lord that was delivered through the prophet Jeremiah but actually destroyed the sacred Scriptures. He was sitting in his winter apartment one morning when several of his assistants brought the scroll on which Jeremiah had written God's words of judgment, which stated that the king of Babylon would attack Jerusalem and destroy it (Jer. 36:28–29). Jehoiakim sat nonchalantly and listened to his right-hand man, Jehudi, read from Jeremiah's scroll. He then deliberately and systematically cut each section from the scroll as it was read and tossed it into his firepot. Piece by piece he destroyed the entire manuscript, openly and flagrantly rejecting God's warnings. We read that "the king and all his attendants who heard all these words showed no fear" (36:24). They would have done well to listen to Solomon's proverb: "The fear of the Lord is the beginning of knowledge, but fools despise wisdom and discipline" (Prov. 1:7). Jehoiakim and his associates demonstrated that they were definitely fools, and they eventually reaped what they had sown!

## *Jerusalem's Doom*

Nebuchadnezzar came to Jerusalem just as Jeremiah had prophesied he would and eventually destroyed the city in 586 B.C. But to understand God's judgment, we need to understand that Nebuchadnezzar's attack on Jerusalem came in three phases. He came first as a general in 605 B.C.—the event described in the opening verses of the book of Daniel (see Fig. 2). Knowing he would soon replace his father as king, he took sacred vessels from the temple and transported them back to Babylon to place them in the house of his own god (Dan. 1:2). At the same time, he transported some of the most intelligent and up-and-coming young men in Judah back to

| Daniel<br>Born | Daniel<br>and<br>Friends<br>Deported | 10,000<br>Jews<br>Deported | Jerusalem<br>Destroyed and<br>the remaining<br>Jews Deported |
|---|---|---|---|
| 620 B.C. ——— | 605 B.C. ——— | 597 B.C. ——— | 586 B.C. |

Fig. 2 - Three Phases In the Babylonian Captivity

his own palace to be thoroughly trained in Babylonian wisdom and culture. Daniel and three close friends were among these young men.

There's an even larger context that helps us understand this first attack on Jerusalem. Egypt, at this time, had already taken control of Jerusalem. In fact, the Egyptian pharaoh, Neco, had actually placed Jehoiakim in power (2 Kings 23:34). Consequently, Nebuchadnezzar first moved against Egypt. Once he had taken control, he then moved his troops toward Jerusalem to make sure Jehoiakim recognized his new political boss.

The opening verse in Daniel reports that Nebuchadnezzar "besieged" Jerusalem. Evidently, Jehoiakim resisted at first but then decided to cooperate and to recognize the king of Babylon as his new supreme commander. In other words, he probably cut a political deal with Nebuchadnezzar and allowed him to have access to some of the sacred vessels in the temple and to take some of Judah's most talented and favorite sons back to Babylon. This would "seal the deal" and explain why Jehoiakim was so sure of himself when Jeremiah prophecied two years later that Nebuchadnezzar would come to Jerusalem and destroy it. In his own mind, Jehoiakim had already made peace with the king of Babylon and felt secure.

Eight years later, however, Nebuchadnezzar—now king of Babylon—attacked Jerusalem a second time (see fig. 2). This time he captured 10,000 Jews and carried them back to Babylon. The author of 2 Kings records that Jehoiakim "changed his mind and rebelled against Nebuchadnezzar"

(2 Kings 24:1). In other words, he arrogantly reneged on his agreement. Consequently, all Judah paid a terrible price.

The relationship between Nebuchadnezzar and the puppet king of Judah continued to deteriorate. Eleven years later, the king of Babylon made his final attack on Jerusalem in 586 B.C. and literally destroyed the whole city—just as Jeremiah had prophesied it would happen (see fig. 2). By this time, Jehoiakim had probably been assassinated and had been succeeded by two kings, Jehoiachin and Zedekiah (see fig. 1). Only a few poverty-stricken people who were not a threat to this Babylonian warlord were allowed to stay in the vicinity of Jerusalem. This final devastating blow ended the reign of the kings of Judah.

## *The King of Kings*

As we reflect on what happened in Israel's history and how all of these events coincide with the history of the other nations of the world, we could conclude that the "one with the most power" wins. There is no question, of course, that Nebuchadnezzar was definitely a great king and a man who commanded a powerful army. But the biblical record clearly states that "the Lord [*Adonai*] delivered Jehoiakim king of Judah into his hand" (Dan. 1:2). Ultimately, God was in control. He used Nebuchadnezzar to bring judgment on Judah, the southern kingdom, just as he had used the Assyrians over a century earlier to bring judgment on Israel, the northern kingdom. Though these pagan leaders believed they were empowered by their own "gods," in actuality they were under the control of the King of kings!

All of this had been prophesied—even before the children of Israel entered the land of Canaan. God had said through Moses:

> *If you fully obey the Lord your God and carefully follow all his commands I give you today, the Lord your God will set you high*

*above all the nations on earth. . . . However, if you do not obey
the Lord your God and do not carefully follow all his commands
and decrees I am giving you today, . . . the Lord will cause you to
be defeated before your enemies. You will come at them from one
direction but flee from them in seven, and you will become a thing
of horror to all the kingdoms on earth (Deut. 28:1, 15, 25).*

Don't misunderstand: Moses' prophecy did not doom
either Israel or Judah to defeat. The Lord had not decreed that
they fail. God's people had a choice—just as Jehoiakim had a
choice when God spoke to him through the prophet Jeremiah.
If he had listened and humbled himself and declared a fast—
a time of mourning for Judah's sins—would God have listened? Of course! He had done it numerous times throughout
Israel's history. But Jehoiakim chose to "spit in God's face." He
scoffed at God and literally destroyed the prophetic Scriptures.
Although he had initially cooperated with Nebuchadnezzar
and "became his vassal," three years later he rebelled, which led
to his untimely death (2 Kings 24:1).

## Becoming God's Man Today

*Principles to Live By*

What can we learn from this initial study in the book of
Daniel? There are several important principles that apply to
our lives.

### *Principle 1. God's promise to Abraham is still unconditional and affects us all.*

Though the children of Israel have been scattered all over the
world, God has not forgotten them. In fact, in 1948, for the
first time since the destruction of Jerusalem by the Romans, the
Jews inherited a homeland—a small section of real estate in the
region where the nation had its birth through Abraham, Isaac,
and Jacob. Many Bible scholars believe this is the beginning of a

very important process in prophetic history where God will literally fulfill His "land promise" to Abraham and his descendants.

However, the most important part of God's promise to Abraham involves "a blessing" for "all peoples on earth" (Gen. 12:2–3). This aspect of the promise was fulfilled in a very specific way when the Lord Jesus Christ came into this world. He was the promised Messiah—the one who would bring blessings to all nations. In Jesus Christ, there are no barriers between Jew and Gentile. When we receive the Lord Jesus Christ as Savior, we are all one in Him. Listen to Paul's words to the Ephesians:

> *For he himself is our peace, who has made the two one [both Jew and Gentile] and has destroyed the barrier, the dividing wall of hostility, by abolishing in his flesh the law with its commandments and regulations. His purpose was to create in himself one new man out of the two, thus making peace, and in this one body to reconcile both of them to God through the cross, by which he put to death their hostility. He came and preached peace to you who were far away [the Gentiles] and peace to those who were near [the Jews]. For through him we both have access to the Father by one Spirit (Eph. 2:14–18).*

### Principle 2. God is still the sovereign Lord and is in control of the universe.

When all is said and done, God is in control of the affairs of all mankind. Even evil and wicked leaders are part of God's divine design. This is illustrated again and again throughout the book of Daniel and that's also why Paul wrote to the Romans and said that "there is no authority except that which God has established" (Rom. 13:1–2).

Paul then became very specific as to what this really means at a practical level:

> *This is also why you pay taxes, for the authorities are God's servants, who give their full time to governing. Give everyone what*

*you owe him: If you owe taxes, pay taxes; if revenue, then revenue; if respect, then respect; if honor, then honor (Rom. 13:6–7).*

As Christians, we have a God-given responsibility to respect those leading us—no matter what their pagan status. Jesus also made this point very clear when He told His followers to "give to Caesar what is Caesar's, and to God what is God's" (Matt. 22:21). Were the Caesars evil men? What many of them did would make the most sinful American president look like a saint. Ultimately, of course, God will hold all government leaders responsible for the evil ways in which they have used their power.

But, you say, as Christians, how far do we carry this principle in our culture? This leads to the next biblical guideline.

*Principle 3. As Christians who form local churches, our primary responsibility is to demonstrate love, unity, and purity throughout a society that is becoming more and more pagan.*

Today, many Christians are confused regarding our primary responsibility as Americans. One reason is that the kind of free society we have in America is not illustrated in Scripture. Furthermore, other than the nation Israel, we have no illustrations of a society built on the values of Scripture like the United States. In this sense, our country is unique.

However, the values in our own society have changed dramatically. Everyone who knows what has happened in our culture since the 1960s acknowledges this reality. Many people who do not hold to the absolute standards of the Bible are delighted. They believe this will lead to a greater America. But those of us who believe the Bible and hold to the ethical and moral principles outlined in the Scriptures are deeply concerned.

And so we should be. Robert H. Bork, in his book entitled *Slouching Towards Gomorrah,* has spoken for all people who hold to the Hebrew-Christian ethic—an ethic upon which our nation was founded. He has written: "Large chunks of the moral life of the United States, major features of its culture, have disappeared altogether, and more are in the process of extinction. These are being, or have already been, replaced by new modes of conduct, ways of thought, and standards of morality that are unwelcome to many of us."[1]

Though Bork does not claim to be an evangelical Christian, he has rightly observed that the "old America" our forefathers once knew and experienced no longer exists. More and more Christians who live today can identify with New Testament believers who came to Christ in a totally pagan culture. Paul succinctly summarized their challenge and responsibility in his letter to the Philippians. They were to "become blameless and pure, children of God without fault in a crooked and depraved generation, in which" they were to "shine like stars in the universe as" they held "out the word of life" (Phil. 2:15–16).

Does this exhortation apply to American Christians? I believe it does—more so than ever before. Our challenge is not to engage in a cultural war, trying to restore what has been lost. What once was is gone. We no longer have leaders in the highest positions in our land who believe and practice biblical values. Furthermore, the majority of Americans seem to believe that a man's personal morals or lack thereof will not negatively affect the way he leads our nation.

There are exceptions, of course. But even a "born again" president who believed that "righteousness exalts a nation, but sin is a disgrace to any people" (Prov. 14:34) would find it very difficult to make any significant changes in our society that would save us from moral and spiritual deterioration. The least he could do would be to slow down the process.

Does this mean we should become pessimistic, fold our hands, and do nothing? Not at all. This leads us to our next principle.

*Principle 4. Within the guidelines of Scripture, we should use every legal right to help restore biblical values*

*in our nation without losing sight of our primary
purpose for being in this world—to carry out the
Great Commission of our Lord Jesus Christ.*

I could hope that we might experience sweeping changes in our culture that reflect the old America—a restoration of family values that are biblical, a reflection of honesty and integrity in our business ethics, a reinstitution of marital values that emphasize a "one-man" and "one-woman" relationship, and a new focus in our entertainment industry that is wholesome and pure. But, in view of both biblical and secular history, such a recovery seldom, if ever, happens in a pluralistic society that has changed its moral direction. However, this should not deter Christians from being dynamic witnesses in the world. We must remember that the darker it becomes, the brighter our light can shine. And one thing is clear from Scripture. As we go about our Father's business, we must not get sidetracked from our primary purpose for living in this world—to bring people to Jesus Christ and to help them live holy and righteous lives. This James calls "pure religion" (James 1:27).

## Personalizing These Principles

What can we do to apply these principles—particularly as they relate to our own culture?

1. Have you presented your body as a living sacrifice to Jesus Christ? Rather than being conformed to this world, are you being transformed (Rom. 12:1, 2)? The place to begin in transforming our society is in our own personal lives.

2. As parents, to what extent is your own "household" in order? Are you following Paul's model in 1 Thessalonians 2:11–12? Our world today desperately needs to see families that are functioning according to God's principles.

3. How much time do you devote to your church? What kind of ministry do you have where you are using your talents and gifts? What percent of your money are you giving to support the ministry of your local church? God has designed the church to be a dynamic force in impacting our local communities with the gospel of Jesus Christ.

4. To what extent are you praying consistently for our government officials? Paul made it very clear that this is a primary responsibility for Christians (see 1 Tim. 2:1–2).

5. To what extent are you aware of what is happening in your community, in your state, and at the national level? Though our citizenship is in heaven, we have a responsibility to be informed as to what is happening in our culture (1 Chron. 12:32).

6. Are you using your rights to vote and to express your opinions at all levels of government? Christians need to use every legal means available to let our voices be heard. We must use our freedoms while we have them, no matter what is happening in our culture.

7. In view of all of your activities, including your political interests, how much time are you devoting to carrying out the Great Commission (Matt. 28:19–20)? Though as Christians we should be good citizens in our country, we must never allow our concerns to sidetrack us from focusing on the real reason God has left us in this world.

### Set a Goal

As you reflect on the principles outlined in this chapter, what one area of personal need has the Holy Spirit brought to your attention? Based on this encounter with the Word of God, write out one specific goal for your own life:

_____

_____

_____

_____

*Memorize the Following Scripture*

> *I urge, then, first of all, that requests, prayers, intercession and thanksgiving be made for everyone—for kings and all those in authority, that we may live peaceful and quiet lives in all godliness and holiness.*

1 Timothy 2:1–2

*Growing Together*

The following questions are designed for small-group discussion:

1. Why is it difficult for Christians to maintain a proper balance between carrying out the Great Commission and attempting to restore biblical values to their rightful place in our society? What do you think this balance is?

2. Do you agree or disagree with the author's perspective on these issues?

3. Why would it be difficult even for a born-again president to change the moral and ethical direction of our society?

4. How do we balance the fact that God is sovereign over the affairs of mankind, yet we are still humanly responsible to take appropriate actions and to be "good citizens" on earth?

5. What can we pray for you personally?

# Chapter 2

# Decisions That Determine Destiny

Read Daniel 1:3–8

$T$he week I was reflecting on Daniel's challenge to live a godly life in a pagan society, I was intrigued by an article in the local newspaper. A Super Bowl champion football player had just returned to the playing field after a five-week suspension. He had been caught in a motel room with two female dancers and illegal drugs. A judge had sentenced him to four years' probation and a number of hours of community service, and the NFL had suspended him from playing for the first five games of the season.

When he came on the field, he was wildly cheered by thousands with only a smattering of boos. After the game, scores of adoring fans crowded around him, attempting to get autographs. One sportswriter asked a fellow player what he thought of the minor negative response from the crowd. "I heard some groans," he said, "but the people who groaned were the ones who never make mistakes."

I admired this interviewer's response. "No," he said, "perhaps some who booed believed strongly that athletes have the responsibility to be role models." He then concluded his article with these very perceptive words—"It's sad but true. Some people value touchdowns more than character."[1]

This story can be multiplied many times in the American society—from the highest office in our land to every nook and cranny of our country. We value many things more than character. In many instances, we just don't care.

By contrast, the story of Daniel is a study in character— from the time we meet him as a teenager (probably around fifteen years old) until he passed off the scene far beyond the age of threescore and ten. He was probably in his mid-eighties.

## High-Level Politics

Nearly twenty years before Jerusalem and Solomon's temple were literally destroyed by the Babylonians, Daniel and a band of other young men in Judah had been taken captive and transported to Babylon to be trained for royal service. After taking control of Egypt, Nebuchadnezzar and his army had marched toward Jerusalem and surrounded the city. Fearing for his life, Jehoiakim, king of Judah, no doubt negotiated a deal, suggesting that Nebuchadnezzar enter the temple of God and select some of the most beautiful and expensive "articles" which he could take back to Babylon and place "in the treasure house" of his own "god" (Dan. 1:2). Furthermore, Daniel and his three friends were certainly part of the deal. They were some of the most brilliant and talented young men in Jehoiakim's own court, and they would make excellent bargaining chips to enable the king of Judah to stay in power over his own people. Evidently, Nebuchadnezzar "shook hands" with Jehoiakim and allowed him to continue in Judah as a vassal king.

## The University of Babylon (1:3–5)

What would you have done at age fifteen if you were forced to enter a pagan school in a foreign country with no choices regarding courses, professors, housing, food, and living arrangements? For most of us who entered college, these were very important personal decisions. But Daniel and a number of other young men had no say in these matters. They were transported to Babylon against their will, and they had no choice but to cooperate. After all, they were put in this difficult position by their own king. To rebel would be to dishonor their own monarch. Furthermore, they would not only have endangered their own lives but the lives of their parents, grandparents, and many other people in Judah.

## The Cream of the Crop

Nebuchadnezzar had extremely high standards for entrance into his highly specialized educational curriculum. Consequently, he "ordered Ashpenaz," who was "chief of his court officials," to select only "some of the Israelites" to enter his program. They were to be "from the royal family and the nobility" (1:3), and since Daniel and his three friends were chosen, it's clear they were not ordinary citizens in Jerusalem. The Jewish historian Josephus theorized they were from the household of Zedekiah (see fig. 1, p. 11), the third son of King Josiah and the last man to serve as king of Judah before Nebuchadnezzar's army destroyed Jerusalem and set fire to Solomon's temple (2 Kings 25:1–7).

These young students were also to be far above average. Physically, they were to be outstanding—free from any defect whatsoever (Dan. 1:4). Their I.Q. scores were to be off the charts—demonstrating an "aptitude for every kind of learning." They were to be "well informed" and "quick to understand." Socially, they were to be "qualified to serve in the king's palace," which means they were well adjusted psychologically with outgoing and appealing personalities. Daniel and his three friends measured up in every respect. They were definitely the "cream of the crop"!

## The Royal Curriculum (1:4–5)

Before they left for Babylon, these young men were already "well informed" regarding Israel's history. But when they arrived in this pagan city, they were introduced to a whole new world of knowledge. Before they could study the volumes of literature in the king's library—which were recorded on clay tablets—they had to learn the Babylonian language.

Learning a foreign language is an incredible challenge in itself, especially when you have to learn it well enough to study highly developed Accadian concepts that included religion, science, and philosophy. As I reflected on Daniel's accomplishments in this arena, I was reminded of my friend, Tolik, who came from the Ukraine to study at Dallas Theological Seminary. He knew just enough English to converse at a rather elementary level. In the next fours years, he became proficient in English and excelled in Greek and Hebrew. When he graduated, he was also honored by being given the distinguished award in theological studies. What an unusual accomplishment!

This kind of aptitude blended with intense determination is mind-boggling. Frankly, my graduate studies stretched my capabilities, and I was listening to lectures and reading books in my native language. Think of the challenge it must have been for Daniel and his three friends to learn a new language so well that they were actually able to excel in their Babylonian studies.

But Nebuchadnezzar's curriculum involved more than academics. He insisted that these young men eat the best food and drink the best wine in the kingdom. Their daily allotment came directly from the king's kitchen. In other words, they ate and drank from the same menu as Nebuchadnezzar.

While enjoying this unique privilege, they must have also "worked out" regularly in the "king's gymnasium," swam laps in his royal swimming pool, and relaxed in his naturally heated saunas. They had an integrated and well-rounded education that money couldn't buy, ate the best food in the kingdom, and lived in an environment that enabled them by age eighteen to become the most outstanding young men in all Babylon—if not in the whole world.

## *Up Close and Personal (1:6–7)*

Though we've already noted that Daniel and his three friends were selected for this high honor, we now meet all four of them personally. Their Hebrew names reflected their religious background. Daniel meant "God is my judge," Hananiah meant "Yahweh is gracious," Mishael "who is what God is?," and Azariah "Yahweh has helped!" (1:6).

To establish new identities for these young men, Ashpenaz assigned all four of them Babylonian names. Though it is difficult to say what each name actually meant, all four new names definitely represented pagan deities. Daniel was renamed Belteshazzar; and Hananiah, Mishael, and Azariah were called Shadrach, Meshach, and Abednego (1:7).

## Daniel's Determination (1:8)

Daniel was definitely the leader among this small band of Israelites. It was he who approached Ashpenaz and sought permission "not to defile himself with the royal food and wine" (1:8). Though Shadrach, Meshach, and Abednego followed suit, Daniel was the one who initially stepped out by faith and took a stand for what he believed was God's will.

### A Godly Heritage

Daniel's decision reflects his godly heritage. These young men were committed to keeping God's laws, even though the majority in Judah were already following false gods when they were taken captive—including their king. Perhaps they had godly mothers and grandmothers who had taught them the Holy Scriptures since the time they were small children—just like Lois and Eunice taught Timothy (2 Tim. 1:5; 3:15).

Whatever the source of their religious education, they knew that the king's food would include meat that the Law of Moses declared unclean (Lev. 11:1–47; Deut. 14:3–20). But more importantly, they knew that the food and wine served them each day had already been dedicated to various pagan deities. To eat and drink would be to publicly acknowledge these false gods. More specifically, Nebuchadnezzar believed that by first offering his food and drink to these gods, he would receive special blessings—physically, mentally, politically, and in other ways. Daniel did not want anyone to conclude that he and his friends had prospered physically, intellectually, and spiritually because the food they ate and the wine they drank had been offered to pagan gods. They did not want these pagan deities to be honored in any way whatsoever.

## A Heart Response

The King James Version reads that "Daniel purposed in his heart that he would not defile himself" (8:1). Literally, this means that Daniel placed this decision "upon his heart." In other words, Daniel knew what was right and wrong. He made a deliberate decision that involved both his head and his heart. Furthermore, his belief regarding keeping the dietary laws of God and avoiding any appearance of idolatry became a very specific conviction regarding the king's food and drink.

## A Bold Decision

Daniel's "heart response" was also a very bold decision. To disobey Nebuchadnezzar could lead to instant death—or at least to serious punishment and possible imprisonment, and incarceration would certainly eliminate any possibility of advancement. Nebuchadnezzar was known throughout the world as a cruel and evil monarch. To cross him, especially under these conditions, could create problems for everyone involved, including Ashpenaz. This unveils another unique quality in Daniel's life.

## Unusual Wisdom

Daniel knew what might happen to his superior should he and his friends refuse to obey the king. He also knew that to resist blatantly would defeat the very purpose he had in mind: to demonstrate that the God of Abraham, Isaac, and Jacob was the one true God. He developed a plan—a wise plan that began with a humble and sensitive approach. Daniel "asked the chief official for permission not to defile himself this way"

(1:8). At this point, he was attempting to practice what Jesus Christ would later declare as being "as shrewd as snakes and as innocent as doves" (Matt. 10:16).

In our next chapter, we'll watch Daniel's plan unfold and see how God blessed his heart decision. But let's stop at this point and look at four very important principles that flow from Daniel's life and which apply to all of us today.

## Becoming God's Man Today

*Principles to Live By*

***Principle 1. If we're going to make deliberate but wise decisions to live in God's will day by day, we must begin with the foundational decision always to honor God with our lives.***

This is why Daniel was able to face the Babylonian culture so decisively. He had already determined to keep God's laws. Long before Paul wrote to the Romans and exhorted them to offer their "bodies as living sacrifices, holy and pleasing to God," Daniel was practicing this truth in his Old Testament setting. He had determined not to conform "to the pattern of this world." He was committed to being "transformed by the renewing" of his mind (Rom. 12:1–2).

If Daniel and his three friends could live this kind of life, how much more should we be able to live in the will of God? We not only understand God's grace in Christ and His wonderful plan of salvation, but we are uniquely indwelt by the Holy Spirit. We have at our disposal "the full armor of God" (Eph. 6:11–18).

Yet this kind of Christian living involves more than simply knowing right from wrong. We must practice the presence of Christ. This is what Paul prayed for the Ephesians—that "Christ may dwell in your hearts through faith" (Eph. 3:17). This is also what Paul meant when he prayed that these Christians might "have power, together with all the saints, to grasp how wide and long and high and deep is the love of Christ, and to know this love that surpasses knowledge—that you may be filled to the measure of all the fullness of God" (3:18–19).

I have personally found that Paul's prayer for the Ephesians is a model prayer for living a victorious Christian life day by day. I often paraphrase this prayer as I apply it to my own life. Try it! And don't forget the marvelous doxology that concludes this prayer: "Now to him who is able to do immeasurably more than all we ask or imagine, according to his power that is at work within us, to him be glory in the church and in Christ Jesus throughout all generations, for ever and ever! Amen" (Eph. 3:20–21).

*Principle 2. When we live and work in an environment that is permeated with values that are out of harmony with God's will, we must make decisions based on God's principles rather than our own legalistic rules.*

Here we can learn a great lesson from Daniel and his three friends. They knew that eating the king's food would violate God's dietary laws—which, of course, are no longer in force today. But for these young men, this was the Law of God. Furthermore, they knew this food was associated with idolatry. They took a stand based on the clear teachings of Scripture.

However, when they were assigned pagan names that were definitely associated with false gods, they did not resist. They knew what their real names meant, and this external change did not affect their hearts or their testimony for God. They could always share personally and privately the true meaning of their Israelite names—perhaps even using their new names as a bridge to share the truth about the God of Abraham, Isaac, and Jacob.

Neither did Daniel and his three friends refuse to study Babylonian subjects, even though they were learning pagan concepts regarding magic and sorcery. They knew what they believed regarding the Law of Moses, and studying these rituals didn't mean they had to practice them. Rather, they were able to interact intelligently and with wisdom as they dialogued with their pagan counterparts. In this sense, they turned "lemons into lemonade"!

Today, some Christians "win battles and lose wars" because they become rigid and legalistic. This is why it's important to understand clearly what the Scriptures really teach so that we are able to make intelligent decisions regarding what is right and wrong and what will honor or dishonor God.

Let me share an example. One day a young man called me very upset. He worked in an office where the employees consumed a lot of alcohol, especially during social events. Wanting to be a witness for Christ, he thought he needed to use this opportunity to announce his commitment to total abstinence. Consequently, he became the object of jokes and derision. People felt uncomfortable around him and began to avoid him.

As we talked, I reminded him that he didn't need to voice his disapproval of their behavior for them to see that he didn't consume alcohol. Rather, he could graciously choose a soft drink rather than booze. Very few people who imbibe judge people who don't. They only resent it when we voice our disapproval.

Suddenly the light went on in this young man's mind. He saw that he could be a much better witness for Christ and open up doors to share the gospel with this kind of attitude.

Please don't misunderstand. I'm not suggesting that we compromise our moral and spiritual convictions. However, I am suggesting that we make wise decisions based on the principles of Scripture rather than our own legalistic rules.

*Principle 3. When we make decisions to take actions that are necessary to avoid compromise, we must always approach our superiors with respect, wisdom, and humility—but realizing we may still pay a price for our stand for righteousness.*

There are definitely times when we must make certain decisions to avoid becoming a part of this world's system. And when we do, we may suffer the consequences. I have a good Christian friend who was in charge of a large investment firm in a well-known bank. On one occasion, an abortion doctor approached him and asked him to invest thousands of dollars. Discovering this was "blood money," my friend decided to refuse this account—literally giving up a $20,000 commission for himself.

The doctor was livid and took the matter directly to the president of the bank. In this case, God honored this man's decision. The president stood behind my friend's decision. Furthermore, in a couple of weeks, another individual approached my friend with a much larger investment. The Lord not only made up the loss but brought in a much larger sum of money.

However, some time later, my friend made another decision. He discovered that one of the accounts he managed was a retirement fund for an organization that circulated pornographic films. Having the authority to make investment decisions, my friend canceled the account.

In this case, the fallout was disastrous. A new president didn't support this decision. Others on staff joined in the attack. My friend stood his ground but paid a painful price for this decision.

Some Christians may conclude that my friend made an unwise decision. After all, the investment had been approved before he took over the responsibility to manage this account. However, he did have the authority to decide what accounts should be opened as well as continued. He did not feel he could in good conscience continue to manage and invest money that had been made on sexually oriented materials.

Whatever your opinion in this matter, God ultimately honored my friend's decision even though it involved a very painful period of time. He kept his job—but only after suffering a lot of persecution. Eventually, however, the Lord opened a unique door for him to launch his own investment business in which he has final responsibility for all accounts. Compared with other companies, he has had unusual success—which seems explainable only by acknowledging that God has blessed this man's willingness to take a stand for righteousness.

When we consider this kind of decision, however, we can learn another great lesson from Daniel. He did so with humility and wisdom. He "sought permission" to refuse to eat the king's food. Furthermore, as we'll see, he proposed a plan that would protect his superior.

I have a brother who is in the concrete business. When he first started, he faced a number of rules and regulations established by the city. As usual, red tape abounded. However, my brother always "went by the book," and never bypassed or violated city ordinances. Today his company is at the top of the list when the city makes recommendations for putting in driveways, curbs, and other city work requirements. He developed trust when other companies lost credibility. It was well worth the extra effort to consult the city officials and to seek their permission before he proceeded. The end result speaks for itself.

## Personalizing These Principles

Meditate on the following Scriptures that illustrate each of the above principles. To what extent are you applying these scriptural truths in your own life?

1. Therefore, I urge you, brothers, in view of God's mercy, to offer your bodies as living sacrifices, holy and pleasing to God—this is your spiritual act of worship. Do not conform any longer to the pattern of this world, but be transformed by the renewing of your mind (Rom. 12:1–2).

2. Be very careful, then, how you live—not as unwise but as wise, making the most of every opportunity, because the days are evil. Therefore do not be foolish, but understand what the Lord's will is (Eph. 5:15–17).

3. So whether you eat or drink or whatever you do, do it all for the glory of God. Do not cause anyone to

stumble, whether Jews, Greeks or the church of God—
even as I try to please everybody in every way. For I am
not seeking my own good but the good of many, so that
they may be saved (1 Cor. 10:31–33).

## Set a Goal

As you've studied these principles and meditated on
God's Word, what specific truth has the Holy Spirit brought
to your attention? Carefully and prayerfully set a specific goal
for your life:

_____

_____

_____

## Memorize the Following Scripture

*I have become all things to all men so that by all possible means*
*I might save some. I do all this for the sake of the gospel, that*
*I may share in its blessings.*
                    1 Corinthians 9:22b, 23

## Growing Together

1. What kind of moral and ethical challenges do you face
   in the workplace?

2. How do you face these challenges and resolve inner
   conflict without compromising your values and creating resentment in your fellow employees?

3. Would you share a situation in which you took a stand
   for righteousness and paid a significant price? Would
   you do the same thing again in the same way?

4. Are there any areas where you believe you are compromising your spiritual values? If so, would you feel free
   to seek wisdom and support from this group?

5. What can we pray for you specifically?

## Chapter 3

# *Making the Best of a Bad Deal*
### Read Daniel 1:9–21

The name Phil Dawson is well known among those who follow college football—especially in the state of Texas. He is best remembered for his game-winning field goal for the Texas Longhorns when they defeated Virginia. It was a 50-yarder—against a 20 m.p.h. wind—and saved Texas's season. "It was probably as big as any single play in our first five years here," commented head coach John Mackovic.

However, prior to this exciting accomplishment, Phil made a decision that in some respects was far more dramatic and significant than his game-winning kick. When chosen by the editors of *Playboy* magazine to be on their pre-season All-American team, he graciously declined! If he had accepted this questionable "honor," he believed his actions would have contradicted the values he had been teaching young men and women who are involved in the organization known as the Fellowship of Christian Athletes.

At first Dawson was nervous about his decision. He was afraid he had alienated his fellow teammates and would appear judgmental. However, he was encouraged 600 letters later, all of which supported this decision. In fact, this positive response from his friends and fans helped him take even bolder steps to share his values with young athletes.

The letter that meant the most came from a prisoner named Shawn Casaday. "I wake up without my family and my freedom each day, all for a compromise in the right thing to do," Casaday wrote. "You have set an example for many behind you, to make the decision for what is right. I personally know, if you compromise, you will regret this decision."[1]

It's refreshing to hear about this kind of young man in today's world. Though Phil Dawson's decision was not nearly as risky or as far reaching as Daniel's, it's an example of a young man who determined in his heart that he would not defile himself by associating with an activity that would denigrate God's name.

## *Full of Grace, Seasoned with Salt*

If your boss or superior in the workplace is not a Christian, what kind of relationship do you have with that person? This is a good question to ask ourselves as we look at Daniel's life in a pagan environment.

After he arrived in Babylon, Daniel was initiated into Nebuchadnezzar's predetermined training program. Though he was a slave, part of his regimen was to "eat like a king"! Nebuchadnezzar ordered Ashpenaz, who was "chief of his court officials," to make sure all those chosen to enter this three-year program ate the same food and drank the same wine served at his royal table.

Daniel had no qualms regarding what he had to study. As long as he didn't have to worship false gods, he didn't resist learning everything he could about them. In fact, he used his inquiring young mind to turn this negative environment into a unique opportunity to expand his own insights so he could interact more intelligently with his secular counterparts. Daniel "jumped in with both feet" and determined to make the best of a bad deal.

### All Truth Is God's Truth

I am reminded of the years I spent working on my Ph.D. at New York University. One of my fellow students was a Christian, and I remember how much he complained about what he felt was a total waste of time studying secular subjects—particularly since some of the information and theories we were learning contradicted the teachings of Scripture. Though I sympathized with my friend, I tried to see it differently—which surprised him. "I'm really enjoying this experience," I said. "It's giving me an opportunity to evaluate secular ideas in the light of the Word of God."

I believe that "all truth is God's truth," no matter where we find it, whether in the Holy Scriptures, which is the divine source of God's revealed truth, or in the arts and sciences, which, of course, is a far less accurate source of truth. However, as a Christian student, this kind of educational experience provided me with an opportunity to build my informational base in order to be a more effective witness for Jesus Christ. It also helped me teach the inspired Word of God in a more relevant fashion.

Daniel must have approached his own learning experience with a positive attitude, even though he would be exposed to ideas that definitely contradicted his own belief system. As we've already noted, Daniel didn't even demonstrate concern over having his Hebrew name changed to Belteshazzar, a pagan name that reflected the pagan gods of the Babylonians. Though he certainly would have preferred keeping his birth name, he didn't feel a name change was worth any kind of resistance in view of other far more important concerns.

## A Line He Could Not Cross

There was an area that deeply troubled Daniel. He was greatly distressed about the king's prescribed meals. Not only would he be forced to violate the dietary laws that God revealed to Moses, but he knew King Nebuchadnezzar's superstitions regarding the food and wine he offered to his pagan gods—namely, that all who ate the food and drank the wine that had first been offered to the pagan gods would prosper physically, intellectually, and spiritually.

Daniel did not want any pagan "gods"—who were not "gods" at all—to receive glory that belonged to God and God alone. He wanted to "abstain from every form of evil"

(1 Thess. 5:22, NKJV)—especially idolatry. Consequently, he resolved ("purposed in his heart") not to defile himself with the royal food and wine (Dan. 1:8).

Because Daniel was a slave and had to be subservient in every way, he knew it would be wise to avoid demonstrating a rebellious spirit. He knew he needed to develop a plan and then wisely and patiently to work that plan. No doubt he initially "ate and drank," but at the same time did everything he could to be a model student. Though the scriptural record makes it very clear that the Lord Himself "caused" Ashpenaz "to show favor and sympathy to Daniel" (1:9), this brilliant young man also developed this trust by doing everything he could to win his "favor and sympathy." Obviously, it took time to build this kind of relationship.

## A Well-Known Example

At this moment in Daniel's life, did he recall another young Israelite who faced a similar predicament? It would be unusual indeed if he had not remembered Joseph's experience when he was sold into Egypt. Every well-taught Jewish boy would have heard this dynamic story, especially his experience in Potiphar's house when he resisted sexual temptation. Daniel certainly was aware of Joseph's successes as well as his trials.

Though "the Lord was with Joseph and he prospered," this young man of seventeen was a faithful and diligent servant. He worked hard to earn Potiphar's trust and eventually was given the responsibility to supervise this powerful and wealthy man's entire household and to manage all of his affairs—which included all of his material possessions (Gen. 39:1–4). After he went to prison because of false accusations, he took the same diligent approach. He was a model prisoner and eventually was given authority over all of the other prisoners (39:20–23).

Following Joseph's example, Daniel also worked hard to win Ashpenaz's trust and support. This is a wonderful Old Testament illustration of applying Paul's words to the Colossian Christians who lived in the midst of a pagan community. "Be wise in the way you act toward outsiders," he wrote; "make the most of every opportunity. Let your conversation be always full of grace, seasoned with salt, so that you may know how to answer everyone" (Col. 4:5–6).

Daniel definitely and wisely made "the most of every opportunity." Consequently, he developed a close friendship with Ashpenaz. People only show "favoritism" when there are emotional ties based on trust, and Ashpenaz's "sympathy" for Daniel definitely indicates a strong relationship with this young man.

## Please Test Your Servants (1:9–13)

What are you willing to trust God for in order to live in His will? Daniel must have thought long and hard about this question and prayed for courage to do the right thing. At some point in time, he decided to take the risk.

Ashpenaz's response demonstrates how risky Daniel's request really was. Though this high-powered official cared about Daniel and respected his desire to want to please his own God, he made it clear he couldn't do anything about Daniel's request. "I am afraid of my lord the king," he responded. "Why should he see you looking worse than the other young men your age? The king would then have my head because of you" (1:10).

Though Ashpenaz cared about and trusted his young friend, he didn't believe his God would cause him to prosper on a substandard diet. He knew that the moment the king noticed that Daniel and his three friends didn't look as healthy as the other young men, he would definitely ask why—which would mean the guillotine for Ashpenaz, "chief of his court officials" or not! Nebuchadnezzar was definitely not a respecter of persons. His word was law, and to violate his will—particularly in this regard—meant instant death!

There is no indication that Daniel pushed—or even pleaded. Though certainly disappointed, he accepted the verdict. In fact, he probably responded with the same courtesy as when he had asked for permission—indicating that he understood Ashpenaz's predicament. However, he had learned a valuable lesson. He'd asked for too much. Consequently, he revised his plan and next approached "the guard" who had been appointed by Ashpenaz to oversee these young men.

Again, it's clear Daniel and his three friends had also developed a trust relationship with this man. This time, however, Daniel presented a very logical, low-risk plan. Approaching the guard with the same courtesy as he had approached Ashpenaz, he requested a short-term trial period: "'Please test your servants for ten days: Give us nothing but vegetables to eat and water to drink. Then compare our appearance with that of the young men who eat the royal food, and treat your servants in accordance with what you see'" (Dan. 1:12–13).

Though violating Nebuchadnezzar's orders in any way could mean sudden death, Daniel's guard was willing to take that risk—which certainly involved Ashpenaz's approval. Ten days of eating vegetables and drinking only water certainly would not cause any appreciable difference in their appearance. Perhaps these two men were simply curious. Possibly they wanted to know more about this God Daniel and his three friends worshiped. Or maybe they simply wanted to end the discussion once and for all.

## *A Great Deal for Everyone (1:13–16)*

Is it possible in a pagan environment to make God-honoring decisions and right choices that will benefit everyone? This certainly isn't always feasible, but it may be possible far more often than we realize if we have the proper perspective on the situation. God may even choose to work a miracle.

What happened next was definitely supernatural. Though a ten-day diet involving water and vegetables would probably help all of us—particularly in terms of weight loss—it wouldn't make the dramatic difference that happened with Daniel and his three friends. "At the end of the ten days they looked healthier and better nourished than any of the young men who ate the royal food" (1:15).

Imagine their guards' initial surprise and consternation when Daniel and his three friends blossomed both physically and intellectually—and only after ten days. The difference had to be substantial and very noticeable to convince him to remove the "choice food and wine they were to drink" on a permanent basis and to give "them vegetables instead" (1:16). This man would never risk his own life for these young Jewish slaves. This was definitely a miracle. Naturally, he would have reported his findings to Ashpenaz.

It wouldn't take Ashpenaz and this unnamed guard long to conclude that this was a great deal. First, if Daniel and his three friends continued to make such incredible progress, this would make both of them look good. Who wouldn't want a "merit badge" from King Nebuchadnezzar?

Furthermore, what happened to the food and wine the guard removed? Ashpenaz and his servant certainly wouldn't have reported their activities to the king, and they definitely wouldn't have requested that the daily meal deliveries cease— since this information would get back to Nebuchadnezzar post haste. To answer this question, we must remember that men who served in this kind of position certainly didn't have access to the king's kitchen as part of their compensation. Consequently, their own families probably "ate like kings" themselves for the next three years. Not a bad deal all the way around!

## God's Special Blessings and Divine Protection (1:17)

Do you believe God will ultimately bless your faith and obedience? At times, this is a difficult question to answer. The fact is that God does bless us, even when we may not experience that reality immediately. His timetable may be quite different from ours, but God will reward us in a special way—even though it may be in eternity. For Daniel and his three friends, the blessings came immediately and throughout their training program.

As time went by, the "risk factor" faded away completely. The Lord gave Daniel and his three friends "knowledge and understanding of all kinds of literature and learning" (1:17). As they diligently studied, they learned faster than their peers. Not only did they stand out physically but intellectually. In addition, God gave Daniel a special spiritual gift: the ability to "understand visions and dreams of all kinds."

God also protected these young men from intellectual and spiritual contamination in spite of their exposure to false and evil information. King Nebuchadnezzar had inherited a remarkable library from the Assyrian emperor, Ashurbanipal (669–626 B.C.). Much of that great source of knowledge included methods of divination—ways to communicate with the unseen world and to determine the will of various gods. Obviously, Daniel studied these methods and understood them thoroughly, but as a God-fearing Jew he never used them. To do so would be to dabble in satanic activity which was strictly forbidden in the Law of Moses (Lev. 19:26).

Ironically, God enabled Daniel to eventually use this exposure to these evil practices to demonstrate God's true power through his own supernatural gift to "understand visions and dreams." In other words, the Lord demonstrated to the Babylonians through Daniel that He was the one true God.

## Graduation with Honors (1:18–21)

In what ways is it possible for Christians to become distinguished and respected leaders in a totally pagan environment? This is not always possible, but Daniel and his three friends demonstrate that with God's help, good things can happen that are beyond our ability to grasp or comprehend.

The time finally came when Daniel and his friends completed the three years of intensive training. Ashpenaz must have been excited, looking forward to this day, knowing that these four young men would stand out, as it were, "head and shoulders" above all the others. And they did! When "the king talked with them . . . he found none equal to Daniel, Hananiah, Mishael and Azariah" (1:19). No one measured up or even came close to their ability to answer questions and provide counsel regarding difficult matters. Whatever the area of knowledge and experience—whether science, language, government, policy, agriculture, art, religion, or military strategy—these young men outdistanced all their peers. In fact, we read that the king "found them ten times better than all the magicians and enchanters in his whole kingdom" (1:20).

Is this hyperbole? In our language, yes. But in the Hebrew language "ten times" may have meant "several" (Zech. 8:23). However, there is another possibility. The word translated "times" literally means "hands." If this is what the text means, then these four young men were equal to "ten hands," or ten people.

Whatever the meaning, it's clear that Daniel and his friends graduated with honors and "entered the king's service" (1:19). They demonstrated much more "wisdom and understanding," not only when compared with the other young men in training but with all the others who had served the king previously as personal counselors. This means they outdistanced men who were much older than they were and who had served the king for years. Intellectually, they were brilliant. Physically, they were without equal. Socially, they handled themselves with ease and poise. Unknown to the king, however, their confidence was in the God whom they loved and trusted, not simply in themselves and not at all in false gods.

At this point in the biblical record, the Holy Spirit transports us ahead many years by informing us "Daniel remained there [in Babylon] until the first year of King Cyrus" (1:21). During this king's first year, Daniel would be over eighty years old. By this time, he would have served in the court of three kings. Although he was not literally a "free man," he became a powerful and respected leader during the seventy years his people were in Babylonian captivity. His spiritual and political influence was enormous.

## Becoming God's Man Today

*Principles to Live By*

*Principle 1. As Christians we should do all we can to win the respect and admiration of non-Christians without compromising our biblical convictions.*

Daniel demonstrated this principle again and again in his own life. He approached his superiors with respect. He sought permission rather than demanding it. He identified with Ashpenaz's hesitancy to grant his request and tried to avoid creating the same tension for his guard.

Following are some New Testament exhortations that underscore this principle:

*Live such good lives among the pagans that, though they accuse you of doing wrong, they may see your good deeds and glorify God on the day he visits us.*

1 Peter 2:12

*But in your hearts set apart Christ as Lord. Always be prepared to give an answer to everyone who asks you to give the reason for the hope that you have. But do this with gentleness and respect, keeping a clear conscience, so that those who speak maliciously against your good behavior in Christ may be ashamed of their slander.*

1 Peter 3:15–16

*Be wise in the way you act toward outsiders; make the most of every opportunity. Let your conversation be always full of grace, seasoned with salt, so that you may know how to answer everyone.*

Colossians 4:5–6

*Principle 2. When taking a public stand for our convictions, we should make sure we're prayerfully and carefully selecting our concerns based on Scripture.*

Again Daniel illustrates this principle in his own life. He could have reacted negatively when his name was changed, refusing to be called Belteshazzar because of its idolatrous associations. He could have refused to study and learn about the evil and satanic practices of the Babylonians. Though these must have been offensive issues to Daniel, he didn't feel they were the concerns he should deal with publicly.

The apostle Paul wrote to the Corinthians, stating that he had "become all things to all men so that by all possible means," he "might save some" (1 Cor. 9:22). This does not mean that Paul compromised his convictions or his public testimony for Christ. He always stood firm on the values of Scripture. However, he did not allow "personal offences" to hinder his ability to be a positive witness for Christ.

For example, I'm always offended when I'm around non-Christians who take the name of Jesus Christ in vain. In fact, all foul language offends me. However, I normally don't feel it would be wise to correct these people, particularly in a public setting. Rather, I try to model language that honors God rather than defames His name, trusting this may give me an opportunity to share the gospel—that "Jesus Christ" is the Son of God and that He died and rose again for all of us so we can live a new life that reflects the values of the Word of God.

While I was putting the finishing touches on this manuscript, Billy Graham had just completed his autobiography entitled *Just As I Am*. With the release of the book, he was interviewed on various prime-time television shows. As always, I was impressed with Billy's ability to respond to controversial questions with wisdom and grace. Without compromising his convictions regarding sin and salvation, he always chose his words carefully so as not to create resentment and negative responses. For example, when challenged about his belief that Jesus Christ was the "only way to heaven," he handled the follow-up question very wisely regarding what would happen to those who follow other religions. He gave a simple response that he believed that God was a righteous judge. This is definitely a biblical answer which was certainly "full of grace and seasoned with salt." Sadly, many Christians try to win little battles and "lose the whole war" in terms of being a positive witness for Jesus Christ.

Don't misunderstand! There are times we can't win "battles" or the "war" when it comes to those who oppose the gospel. The religious leaders particularly hated Jesus Christ and the apostles as well. However, much of their hatred was based on the fact that their own disciples were transferring their loyalties to the Savior. In general, the New Testament church "had favor" with ordinary people (Acts 2:47).

Obviously, it takes wisdom to know how to speak and when to remain silent—wisdom that God wants to give us so that we, like Daniel, can make "the most of every opportunity" (Eph. 5:16).

### Principle 3. When taking a public stand in order not to compromise our spiritual convictions, we must trust God for His supernatural assistance.

As Christians, we're engaged in a spiritual battle. Paul wrote that "our struggle is not against flesh and blood, but against the rulers, against the authorities, against the powers of this dark world and against the spiritual forces of evil in the heavenly realms" (Eph. 6:12). This is why we must "be strong in the Lord and in his mighty power" (6:10).

We must not try to tackle spiritual issues in our own strength. True, we are to use all of the natural abilities and skills God has given us, but when all is said and done, the "battle is the Lord's." This was King David's testimony when he went out to confront Goliath. Though he could use a slingshot like no other young man, he still knew that to win the battle against this wicked man, he needed God's strength.

The principle is clear. Unfortunately, we often don't trust God as we should to help us and to protect us, and to use us to be a dynamic witness in the secular world.

*Principle 4. When we make every effort to do God's will,*
*He will eventually bless us for our faithful obedience.*

This does not mean we'll never face rejection, persecution, and pain. The Lord never promised us we would be free from trials and tribulation. However, He will never forsake us. Sometimes blessings are immediate and very obvious, as they were with Daniel and his three friends. At other times, the blessings may be delayed. But we can be sure they will always come—sometimes in ways we don't even recognize. Obedience does bring blessings—even in the midst of difficult circumstances. And of course the most significant rewards will come when we're face to face with Jesus Christ and hear Him say, "Well done, good and faithful servant."

## Personalizing These Principles

The following questions will help you evaluate your own witness to others:

1. What are you doing specifically to win the respect and admiration of non-Christians—your boss, your fellow employees, your professors, your classmates, your unsaved neighbors?

2. What decisions have you made to be separate from the world that may be hurting your witness for Jesus Christ? Conversely, what decisions have you made that have compromised your spiritual convictions?

3. To what extent are you trusting God to assist you in your witness for Christ? On the other hand, in what ways have you neglected your human responsibility to build bridges to unsaved people?

4. To what extent do you believe God will honor your faithful obedience? What evidences can you point to

that demonstrate that you believe He will reward you—either in this present world or in eternity?

## Set a Goal

As you reflect on these principles outlined in this chapter and the way you have or have not personalized them, ask the Lord to show you what one goal you need to set for your life:

_____

_____

_____

## Memorize the Following Scripture

*Trust in the Lord with all your heart and lean not on your own understanding; in all your ways acknowledge him, and he will make your paths straight.*

Proverbs 3:5–6

## Growing Together

1. What are some of the roadblocks you face in winning the respect and admiration of the non-Christians you rub shoulders with on a regular basis?

2. What are some of the areas Christians take a stand against in the secular environment that should be secondary issues, thus hindering their witness?

3. Why do we find it difficult to maintain a proper balance in trusting God to help us resolve problems in our relationships and in trying to work it out in our own strength? What steps have you taken personally to maintain this balance?

4. How has God rewarded you for taking a stand for righteousness? On the other hand, what price have you had to pay?

5. What can we pray for you specifically?

Chapter 4

# A Mysterious Drama
### Read Daniel 2:1–49

*T*he next event in the Book of Daniel reads like a powerful five-act drama that spans the course of human history.
With a series of dreams, the sovereign God invaded the heart
and mind of a pagan tyrant, King Nebuchadnezzar. In these
dreams, the Lord outlined a rather detailed picture of what
would happen in the future. The king, however, was terribly
confused and deeply troubled. He had no earthly idea as to
what his dreams really meant.

Before we pull the curtain on Act I, let's listen to our
Divine Narrator set the stage:

> *In the second year of his reign, Nebuchadnezzar had dreams;*
> *his mind was troubled and he could not sleep. So the king sum-*
> *moned the magicians, enchanters, sorcerers and astrologers to tell*
> *him what he had dreamed (Dan. 2:1–2a).*

## Act I

### Troubling Dreams and Nebuchadnezzar's Frustration (2:3–11)

THE KING: I have had a dream that troubles me and
I want to know what it means.

THE ASTROLOGERS: O king, live forever! Tell your servants
the dream, and we will interpret it.

---

48

| | |
|---|---|
| THE KING: | This is what I have firmly decided: If you do not tell me what my dream was and interpret it, I will have you cut into pieces and your houses turned into piles of rubble. But if you tell me the dream and explain it, you will receive from me gifts and rewards and great honor. So tell me the dream and interpret it for me. |
| THE ASTROLOGERS: | Let the king tell his servants the dream, and we will interpret it. |
| THE KING: | I am certain that you are trying to gain time, because you realize that this is what I have firmly decided: If you do not tell me the dream, there is just one penalty for you. You have conspired to tell me misleading and wicked things, hoping the situation will change. So then, tell me the dream, and I will know that you can interpret it for me. |
| THE ASTROLOGERS: | There is not a man on earth who can do what the king asks! No king, however great and mighty, has ever asked such a thing of any magician or enchanter or astrologer. What the king asks is too difficult. No one can reveal it to the king except the gods, and they do not live among men. |

As we reflect on this very dramatic interchange between Nebuchadnezzar and his counselors, note several things. First, the king must have had recurring "dreams" (2:1a), but it was the same dream. This is why he spoke of a single dream when he spoke to his wise men (1:3).

Second, before Nebuchadnezzar even called these men to appear before him, he had already made up his mind that he was going to command them not only to interpret this strange dream but to reveal what it was!

Third, Nebuchadnezzar was already intensely angry. His penalty for his astrologers' inability to respond in the way he had asked didn't match the crime. He had determined ahead of time to destroy all of his best men and to level their homes (2:5).

Why this bizarre behavior? Was this simply a result of his frustration in not being able to understand this recurring dream? I don't think so. Nebuchadnezzar had definitely become suspicious that his so-called "wise men" were not as "wise" as they claimed to be (2:6b). This may be why he accused them of conspiring to report to him "misleading and wicked things" (2:9). This strong indictment seems to reflect an intense lack of trust that had either been building over a period of time or perhaps resulted from something that had just happened that we're not told about.

Whatever the circumstances, Nebuchadnezzar was so irate and offended he was out of control. This would be like the president of the United States ordering a death sentence for every member of Congress—and then commanding their assassins to use bulldozers to level the homes they lived in!

Nebuchadnezzar's magicians, enchanters, sorcerers, and astrologers were trapped. If they had been truly wise, they would have admitted any conspiracy and misleading behavior, bowing low before the king and begging for mercy. Instead, they accused Nebuchadnezzar of being unfair. They tried to cover their own mistakes by blaming the king—which was their biggest mistake!

## Act II

### Nebuchadnezzar's Decree and Arioch's Explanation (2:12–16)

The next scene in this unfolding drama is even more intense. Nebuchadnezzar's anger reached a fever pitch. He followed through on what he had threatened and "ordered the execution of all the wise men of Babylon" (2:12).[1] Included on this "hit list" were Daniel and his three friends (2:13).

What happened next introduces us to a new dimension for speculation. Note first that Nebuchadnezzar had his recurring dream in the second year of his reign (2:1). Since he replaced his father as king shortly after he took Daniel and his three friends captive and ordered that they be taught the Babylonian language and introduced to Babylonian literature, this means that these young men had probably already entered an apprenticeship program before they had completed the three-year curriculum. In other words, Daniel, Hananiah, Mishael, and Azariah had already been placed in influential positions. Even though they were still interns and not full-fledged "wise men," they were still included among those to be assassinated.

However, what happened next indicates that Daniel had already won the trust of the king and Arioch, who served as "commander of the king's guard" (2:14). If he had not, why would this powerful official—who was probably Nebuchadnezzar's own bodyguard—come to Daniel's quarters? After all, these young men were only "wise men in training."

Furthermore, why would Arioch even listen to Daniel's questions regarding Nebuchadnezzar's harsh decree and then take time to explain what had happened? More importantly, why would young Daniel be granted an audience with Nebuchadnezzar?

This raises an even more intriguing question. Is it possible that it was Daniel and his three friends who had sowed seeds of doubt in Nebuchadnezzar's mind regarding his own pagan wise men and their false motives and tricky methods? Perhaps the openness and honesty of these young men from Judah had given Nebuchadnezzar a basis for comparison. Had Daniel already distinguished himself as a young man who could "understand visions and dreams of all kinds" (1:17)?

If this interpretation of what happened is true, it helps explain rather clearly Nebuchadnezzar's bizarre behavior, why

Arioch personally appeared in Daniel's quarters, and why he took time to explain what had precipitated Nebuchadnezzar's harsh decree. Most importantly, it helps explain why young Daniel—who was not even an official counselor—had a private audience with King Nebuchadnezzar and actually convinced him to stay the execution and to give him time to discover both what the dream was and what it meant. Obviously, Arioch had built this bridge to the king, but he did so because he knew Daniel had a supernatural gift to interpret dreams and visions.

## Act III

### Four Men's Prayers and Daniel's Adoration (2:17–23)

When Daniel left the king's quarters, he wasted no time taking action. First, he hurriedly explained everything to Hananiah, Mishael, and Azariah (2:17). Next, he called an urgent prayer meeting and asked them to join him in pleading "for mercy from the God of heaven" regarding the king's mysterious dreams.

We're not told how much time Nebuchadnezzar gave Daniel, but in view of Daniel's urgent report and request for prayer, it may have been only twenty-four hours. These young men were living on borrowed time. Nebuchadnezzar's anger could explode into action at any moment. Daniel knew that if God did not immediately reveal both the dream and what it meant, he and his three friends were doomed to die "with the rest of the wise men of Babylon" (2:18).

God honored these four young men's plea for mercy. He answered their prayers that very night. By morning, Daniel knew the dramatic details of the dream and what they actully meant.

Daniel still had to move quickly in this life-and-death situation. But before he reported the revelation and interpretation to the king, he paused long enough to lift his voice to

God in a prayer of praise and thanksgiving. His words speak for themselves:

> *Praise be to the name of God for ever and ever;*
> *wisdom and power are his.*
> *He changes times and seasons;*
> *he sets up kings and deposes them.*
> *He gives wisdom to the wise*
> *and knowledge to the discerning.*
> *He reveals deep and hidden things;*
> *he knows what lies in darkness,*
> *and light dwells with him.*
> *I thank and praise you, O God of my fathers:*
> *You have given me wisdom and power,*
> *you have made known to me what we asked of you,*
> *you have made known to us the dream of the king (2:20–23).*

The focus of this prayer and praise is clearly on God and His "wisdom and power." Daniel took absolutely no credit for what had just happened. He gave all glory and praise to God. Including proper nouns and pronouns, Daniel referred to the Lord thirteen times and used only five pronouns to refer to himself and to his three friends. Even then, the focus is still on God as the source of all that had happened. What incredible maturity for a young man of seventeen.

## *Act IV*

### *Divine Mysteries and Daniel's Interpretation (2:24–45)*

Following his prayer of praise, Daniel went directly to Arioch and asked him not to proceed with the execution. He then asked this chief officer to escort him to the king so he could reiterate the details in the dream and explain the meaning (2:24).

Arioch's response adds another key in interpreting earlier events in this intense drama. He reported to the king that he had discovered Daniel—"a man among the exiles from Judah who can tell the king what his dream means" (2:25).

When Arioch once again introduced Daniel to Nebuchadnezzar, there is no indication that the king ever questioned Arioch's self-promotional maneuver for taking credit for discovering Daniel. After all, the king honored men who could outsmart each other. Rather, he immediately directed a question at Daniel, asking him if he could both tell him what he "saw" in the dream and what it meant (2:26).

Before Daniel revealed the details of the dream to Nebuchadnezzar, he established a very important point. He underscored the truth that got the king's wise men into trouble in the first place—that "no wise man, enchanter, magician or diviner" could "explain to the king the mystery" (2:27a). "But," Daniel continued, "there is a God in heaven who reveals mysteries. He has shown King Nebuchadnezzar what will happen in days to come" (2:28). (See fig. 3.)

## Act V

### The King's Honor and Daniel's Elevation (2:46–49)

When Nebuchadnezzar heard Daniel recreate the specific details of the dream and then explain what these details meant as illustrated in figure 3, he was astonished and overwhelmed. He was so overcome with awe that he "fell prostrate before Daniel and paid him honor," and then commanded his servants to present Daniel with an "offering and incense" (2:46). There was no question in his mind that this was a supernatural feat!

Nebuchadnezzar then made a public statement that must have overwhelmed Daniel, his three friends, and all of his own wise men: "Surely your God is the God of gods, and the Lord of kings and a revealer of mysteries, for you were able to reveal this mystery" (2:47). Though Nebuchadnezzar did not reject his pagan gods, he at least acknowledged that Daniel's God was more powerful than any "god" he had ever worshiped.

At some point following this dramatic moment in Daniel's life, Nebuchadnezzar presented this young man with "many gifts" and then promoted him to "a high position" in the kingdom. In fact, "he made him ruler over the entire province of Babylon." Furthermore, he "placed him in charge of all its wise men" (2:48).

Daniel once again revealed his true character when he approached the king and recommended that his three friends—Shadrach, Meshach, and Abednego—be appointed as key administrators over the province. Nebuchadnezzar responded positively and assigned them to locations in his kingdom. However, "Daniel himself remained at the royal court" (2:49).

We're not told how quickly all of this happened. Perhaps the king allowed Daniel and his three friends to complete their training program since they did not officially enter

## THE KING'S DREAM

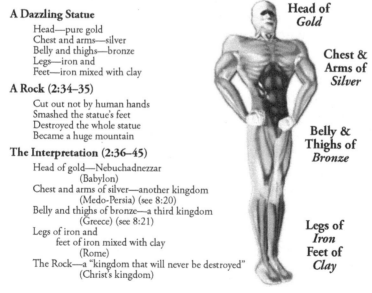

**A Dazzling Statue**

Head—pure gold
Chest and arms—silver
Belly and thighs—bronze
Legs—iron and
Feet—iron mixed with clay

**A Rock (2:34–35)**

Cut out not by human hands
Smashed the statue's feet
Destroyed the whole statue
Became a huge mountain

**The Interpretation (2:36–45)**

Head of gold—Nebuchadnezzar
     (Babylon)
Chest and arms of silver—another kingdom
     (Medo-Persia) (see 8:20)
Belly and thighs of bronze—a third kingdom
     (Greece) (see 8:21)
Legs of iron and
     feet of iron mixed with clay
     (Rome)
The Rock—a "kingdom that will never be destroyed"
     (Christ's kingdom)

Head of
*Gold*

Chest &
Arms of
*Silver*

Belly &
Thighs of
*Bronze*

Legs of
*Iron*
Feet of
*Clay*

**Fig. 3 - Nebuchadnezzar's Dream and Daniel's Interpretation**

"the king's service" until that point in time (1:19). However, even if Nebuchadnezzar waited a full year before making these appointments, Daniel and his friends would have been only eighteen years old! It's difficult to imagine four teenagers with this kind of authority. However, because they had prayerfully handled God's divine power with wisdom, tact and humility, they were able to handle Nebuchadnezzar's human power with the same spirit. Though the Lord had sovereignly designed this plan, Daniel and his friends had diligently prepared themselves for this moment in world history—physically, intellectually, and, most of all, spiritually. In God's timing, He used their human talents and their diligence to achieve His divine purposes.

## Becoming God's Man Today

*Principles to Live By*

*Principle 1. Though God is sovereign and in control of history, He has chosen to use our human knowledge, wisdom, tact, and abilities to achieve His divine and eternal purposes (Acts 4:23–31; Rom. 11:33–36).*

This in itself is a divine mystery. Who can understand it? People have tried to explain it but always fail. They either go to one extreme or the other—either emphasizing God's sovereignty and neglecting man's responsibility or emphasizing man's free will and failing to give a proper place to God's preordained plans. I prefer to leave this where Paul left it in his letter to the Romans. After dealing with the sovereignty of God in chapters 9, 10, and 11, he exclaimed:

> *Oh, the depth of the riches of the wisdom and knowledge of God! How unsearchable his judgments, and his paths beyond tracing out!*

> *Who has known the mind of the Lord?*
> *Or who has been his counselor?*
> *Who has ever given to God, that God should repay him?*
> *For from him and through him and to him are all things.*
> *To him be the glory forever! Amen (Rom. 11:33–36).*

*Principle 2. Though God is sovereign, He has chosen to use the process of prayer to unleash His miraculous power to enable us to solve problems that range from those simple issues we face at the purely human level to those that are very complex and far beyond our human capabilities.*

That the sovereign God responds to our prayers is an extension of this divine mystery. When we pray, it makes a difference! Dick Eastman states: "Somehow, the simple act of prayer links the sovereign God to a finite man. When man prays, God responds. Difficult situations change. Unexpected miracles occur."[2]

Elaborating on this concept even further, E. Stanley Jones explains:

> *In prayer you align yourself to the purpose and power of God, and He is able to do things through you that He couldn't do otherwise. For this is an open universe, where some things are left open, contingent upon our doing them. If we do not do them, they will never be done, for God has left certain things open to prayer—things which will never be done except as we pray.[3]*

*Principle 3. No matter how much we contribute to God's work in this world with our time, our talents, and our treasures, we should always give Him all honor and glory for what has been accomplished (Eph. 3:20–21).*

Daniel had one main concern—that God's name be lifted up and exalted. Obviously, he knew he was intelligent and had an outgoing personality and a good self-image. But he also knew that God deserved all the glory for anything that he accomplished. This is why he approached the king with these words: "As for me, the mystery has been revealed to me, not because I have greater wisdom than other living men, but so that you, O king, may know the interpretation . . ." (2:30). Daniel's humility is amazing. Most eighteen-year-olds would have been so filled with pride they would have done anything possible to demonstrate to the king how smart and intelligent they were. But not Daniel. He wanted God to be honored and glorified above all.

It's refreshing and encouraging that Daniel maintained this attitude and spirit all of his life. He made a great start and had a great finish.

## Personalizing These Principles

The following questions and Scriptures will help you apply these principles in your day-to-day living:

1. How available are you to God to use your knowledge and wisdom, abilities and gifts to achieve His eternal purposes in this world?

   *Consider Paul's grand doxology in his letter to the Ephesians: "Now to him who is able to do immeasurably more than all we ask or imagine, according to his power that is at work within us, to him be glory in the church and in Christ Jesus throughout all generations, for ever and ever! Amen."*

   Ephesians 3:20–21

2. To what extent do you practice the privilege of prayer to unleash God's power in your life and to help you accomplish things that are beyond your natural capabilities?

   *Consider Paul's encouraging exhortation to the Philippian Christians: "Do not be anxious about anything, but in*

*everything, by prayer and petition, with thanksgiving, present your requests to God. And the peace of God, which transcends all understanding, will guard your hearts and your minds in Christ Jesus."*
Philippians 4:6–7

3. When God responds to your prayers and uses your abilities and gifts to achieve His divine purposes, are you able to honor and glorify Him rather than taking credit for yourself?

*Consider Paul's words to the Roman Christians: "For by the grace given me I say to every one of you: Do not think of yourself more highly than you ought, but rather think of yourself with sober judgment, in accordance with the measure of faith God has given you."*
Romans 12:3

### Set a Goal

Review the principles in this chapter, asking the Holy Spirit to reveal one area in your life that needs immediate attention. Then set a specific goal, asking God to enable you to achieve that goal:

_____

_____

_____

### Memorize the Following Scripture

*Oh, the depth of the riches of the wisdom and knowledge of God! How unsearchable his judgments, and his paths beyond tracing out!*
Romans 11:33

### Growing Together

1. Why is it easy for Christians to go to one extreme or the other in trying to resolve what appears to be a tension between God's sovereign control of the events in

human history and our responsibility to help change the course of human history?

2. How is the subject of prayer related to this great mystery? In other words, why should we pray if God is in sovereign control of the universe?

3. Why is it so easy for all of us to take credit for things that we've accomplished rather than to glorify God?

4. How do we balance feeling good about ourselves and our accomplishments while honoring God and thanking Him for enabling us to succeed in life? In other words, how do we avoid demonstrating "false humility"?

5. What can we pray for you specifically?

# Chapter 5

# *Tried by Fire*
Read Daniel 3:1–30

When my wife and I were in Rome, we walked through the huge amphitheater where many Christians lost their lives because they refused to deny their allegiance to Jesus Christ. Polycarp, a disciple of the apostle John, was one of those early Christian martyrs. When ordered to renounce his faith and worship the Roman emperor, Polycarp responded before a roaring crowd of spectators, "Eighty and six years have I served Him, and He never did me any injury: how then can I blaspheme my King and my Savior?"

At this point, the official in charge threatened him with wild beasts that were ready to be released from their cages. But Polycarp answered, "Call them then, for we are not accustomed to repent of what is good in order to adopt that which is evil; and it is well for me to be changed from what is evil to what is righteous."

Seeing Polycarp's determination not to turn his back on Jesus Christ, his would-be executioner threatened to burn him at the stake. But again, this great man of God responded, "Thou threatenest me with fire which burneth for an hour, and after a little is extinguished, but art ignorant of the fire of the coming judgment and of eternal punishment, reserved for the ungodly. But why tarriest thou? Bring forth what thou wilt."[1]

Over the centuries, many of God's children have faced serious persecution for their faith. Some have been marvelously and miraculously delivered from death, but some have given their lives and have been delivered into the presence of God (Heb. 11:36–39a).

As Christians down through the centuries have faced death for refusing to deny Jesus Christ as their Lord and Savior, I'm confident that many of them vividly remembered what happened to Daniel's three friends—young men who were thrown into a fiery furnace because they refused to bow down and worship a huge statue constructed by King Nebuchadnezzar. In this instance, these young men were miraculously delivered from physical death because of their faith. As we'll see, they were also willing to die! They had no knowledge that God was going to preserve them until they were in the midst of the roaring flames.

## Self-centered Gratification (3:1–6)

As time passed by, Nebuchadnezzar conveniently forgot his dramatic experience when Daniel supernaturally reiterated and interpreted his dream (2:29–45). The king was so overwhelmed that he willingly and humbly acknowledged that Daniel's God was "the God of gods and the Lord of kings and a revealer of mysteries" (2:47). But only two or three years later, he "made an image of gold, ninety feet high and nine feet wide, and set it up on the plain of Dura in the province of Babylon" (3:1). He then issued an order that all of his important officials throughout the cou try come together for a special "dedication of the image" (3:3). As they all stood before this gigantic monument that towered high above them, they were commanded to "fall down and worship" the image (3:6). The signal to prostrate themselves would be the first notes from a grand overture played by the Babylonian symphony (3:5). To refuse to bow down meant an instant and fiery death in "a blazing furnace" (3:6).

When Nebuchadnezzar had been reigning as king for only four or five years, he already had become the world's greatest emperor, which was symbolized "by the head of gold" in his earlier dream (2:38). He had conquered "peoples, nations and men of every language" (3:4). But to rule was not enough. He wanted to be worshiped, which was symbolized by this huge statue.

We must understand that Nebuchadnezzar had never given up the worship of his pagan gods. When Daniel had interpreted his dream a couple of years earlier, he simply acknowledged that Daniel's "god" was a "greater god" than his own. He did not experience a true conversion to the God of Abraham, Isaac, and Jacob. In fact, as time went by, he may have been threatened as people began to respect Daniel and his three friends whom he had placed in high positions throughout the province of Babylon.

## *Immediate Deification (3:7)*

Whatever reason Nebuchadnezzar had in constructing this huge statue, his arrogance was personified as it towered high above the desert floor. Everyone who witnessed what was happening knew beyond a shadow of a doubt that he meant business. They could hear the roar of flames in the background! Consequently, when Nebuchadnezzar's orchestra began to play, "all the peoples, nations and men of every language fell down and worshiped the image of gold that King Nebuchadnezzar had set up" (3:7).

Though there must have been hundreds—some believe thousands—of people present for this incredible event, three young Israelites stood out in the crowd. When all of Nebuchadnezzar's servants were flat on their faces—for fear they would be in violation of the king's order—Daniel's friends remained standing. They would not bow down to this great image. Clearly it would be a violation of the law that God gave to Moses at Mount Sinai. The Lord had made it clear that no person in Israel was to engage in this kind of idolatry. God had thundered from the holy mountain the following specific exhortations:

*"You shall not make for yourself an idol in the form of anything in heaven above or on the earth beneath or in the waters below. You shall not bow down to them or worship them; for I, the Lord your God, am a jealous God, punishing the children for the sin of the fathers to the third and fourth generation of those who hate me, but showing love to a thousand generations of those who love me and keep my commandments" (Exod. 20:4–6).*

Shadrach, Meshach, and Abednego knew only too well that they had been carried into Babylonian captivity because their fathers and forefathers had violated the Lord's commands and had worshiped the gods of Canaan. They were determined to break this cycle of idolatry in Israel. Clearly, they were willing to face Nebuchadnezzar's temporal punishment rather than to face their eternal God and have to give account for the sin of idolatry.

## Jealous Retaliation (3:8–12)

There they stood—and they were quickly noticed. A group of astrologers (or Chaldeans) quickly reported what had happened. "There are some Jews," they said, "whom you have set over the affairs of the province of Babylon—Shadrach, Meshach, and Abednego—who pay no attention to you, O king. They neither serve your gods nor worship the image of gold you have set up" (3:12).

These men were probably ecstatic at the opportunity to report this information to Nebuchadnezzar. After all, these young men—who were probably only about twenty years old at the time—had been appointed by the king to serve in significant administrative positions in the province of Babylon. What an opportunity to vent their feelings of jealousy.

Remember too that Daniel had become "ruler over the entire province of Babylon" and the king also "placed him in charge of all its wise men"—which would have included the men who reported this latest information to the king (2:48). There's no question these astrologers would resent all four of these young men and relish the opportunity to gain some "brownie points" with the king—and in the process, get rid of at least three of them.

This raises an interesting question. Where was Daniel? In answering this question, we can only speculate. Perhaps his high position of power exempted him from having to attend this event. After all, he was "ruler over the entire province of Babylon." Knowing what was about to happen, he may have simply remained in the king's court and no one would question his decision—including the king. After all, he was no ordinary official. It's also possible, of course, that he was on the king's business somewhere else in the province.

## *Reluctant Reconsideration (3:13–15)*

Once Nebuchadnezzar heard about Shadrach, Meshach, and Abednego, he went into a rage. He was furious—and not for the first time. We saw this kind of temper tantrum several years before when his wise men had been unable to interpret his dream, and in a fit of frenzy and uncontrolled anger, he issued an order that they all be killed including Daniel and his three friends (2:12–13).

Nevertheless, Nebuchadnezzar was still objective enough to give Shadrach, Meshach, and Abednego another chance. After all, they were some of his most valued officials. On the other hand, his pride kept him from exonerating them and giving them permission to refuse to worship his image. Consequently, he restated the penalty for failing to abide by his order. "If you do not worship it," he stated, "you will be thrown immediately into a blazing furnace. Then what god will be able to rescue you from my hand?" (3:15).

## *Consistent Determination (3:16–18)*

Shadrach, Meshach, and Abednego bravely stood their ground, knowing full well the consequences that lay ahead!

Even though divine politics had been one of their hall-marks ever since they were brought to Babylon, there comes a moment in time when all of the "wisdom and tact" in the world will no longer work in relating to evil people. Shadrach, Meshach, and Abednego had reached that point. Any other approach would compromise their faith and their relationship with the one true God. Their response was straightforward—and a great witness to their commitment to the Lord:

> *"Nebuchadnezzar, we do not need to defend ourselves before you in this matter. If we are thrown into the blazing furnace, the God we serve is able to save us from it, and He will rescue us from your hand, O king. But even if he does not, we want you to know, O king, that we will not serve your gods or worship the image of gold you have set up" (3:16–18).*

## Unusual Antagonism (3:19–23)

Nebuchadnezzar had calmed down during his conversation with Shadrach, Meshach and Abednego. Down deep, he surely didn't want to destroy these young men who had served him so faithfully. But their uncompromising response once again ignited his intense and irrational anger. No doubt deeply threatened, he became infuriated. His whole countenance changed. In a state of near irrationality, he ordered the furnace stoked and "heated seven times hotter than usual" (3:19).

Though Nebuchadnezzar may have been using hyperbole, it certainly indicates that he wanted to prove that he was more powerful than the "god" these three men worshiped and served. It appears he had not forgotten completely his proclamation several years before—that these young men's God was "the Lord of kings" (2:47). He desperately wanted to win this battle—and prove once and for all that his power was greater than any "foreign god." If he were not fearful and threatened, why then would he have to make the fire so hot? After all, a normal fire will destroy anything in its path—especially human beings who have no way to protect themselves.

But Nebuchadnezzar took every precaution. He had these men "firmly tied," bound hand and foot. He wanted to make any form of escape impossible, which is also why he must have ordered his soldiers to come so close to the furnace before they released these three young men. And when they did, the flames literally leaped from this burning inferno and ignited their clothes, burning them to death.

## Instant Consternation (3:25–26)

Ironically, Nebuchadnezzar's men were destroyed by only coming close to the fire, and Shadrach, Meshach, and Abednego were still alive in the midst of the flames. The king recognized immediately that something supernatural had happened. He saw not only three men standing in the midst of the roaring fire but four. He also recognized that the fourth person was no ordinary human being. "Look!" he shouted. "I see four men walking around in the fire, unbound and unharmed, and the fourth looks like a son of the gods" (3:25).

## Divine Preservation (3:27)

Unknown to Nebuchadnezzar, he was viewing an Old Testament manifestation of the one and only Son of God. This was no ordinary angel. This was the angel of the Lord—an Old Testament manifestation of Jesus Christ.

Since these men were already "unbound" as they stood in the midst of the fire, Nebuchadnezzar ordered them to come out of the furnace. No servant dared help them since they would also be destroyed by the blazing fire. On their own, Shadrach, Meshach, and Abednego stepped from the fiery inferno, untouched by the flames. The angel of the Lord—who had completed his task—disappeared.

Absolutely amazed, all of Nebuchadnezzar's men crowded around these young men. Imagine the sense of awe when they observed that Shadrach, Meshach, and Abednego had no scars whatsoever. Their skin tones were normal. Not even the hair on their heads was singed. Their official robes were as neatly pressed and as colorful as the moment they put them on that morning. They didn't even smell like smoke. Once again, Nebuchadnezzar had come face to face with the living God and a miracle of His grace.

## A Universal Declaration (3:28–29)

What could Nebuchadnezzar do at this moment but worship the one true God? He had been soundly defeated. What impacted him the most was that Shadrach, Meshach, and Abednego "were willing to give up their lives rather than to serve or worship any god except their own God" (3:28). Consequently, Nebuchadnezzar once again did an "about face," going from one extreme to the other. He issued another order—a "decree that the people of any nation or language who say anything against the God of Shadrach, Meshach, and Abednego be cut into pieces and their houses be turned into piles of rubble" (3:29). Nebuchadnezzar recognized that "no other god can save in this way."

## Another Ironic Elevation (3:30)

The officials who jealously tried to destroy these young men by reporting their behavior to Nebuchadnezzar only ended up helping them get promoted and elevated to even greater positions in the province of Babylon. What an ironic twist to this dramatic story. Even the Lord must have "smiled."

Shadrach, Meshach, and Abednego's reactions are not described. However, it doesn't take much imagination to conclude that their love for God was even greater than before. They must have served Him with a new sense of commitment and dedication, realizing that the Lord had spared them for a unique purpose.

Needless to say, part of that purpose had already been unveiled. Think of the impact this experience had on all of the wise men and chief officials in Babylon. If they said one negative thing about the God of Israel, they would be eliminated. Outwardly, at least, they had to acknowledge the one true God. What happened inwardly we're not told. But one thing is certain: God had once again revealed His glory to some of the most significant unbelievers in the world. Furthermore, He did it through three twenty-year-old men who were determined to serve and worship God and Him alone.

## Becoming God's Man Today

*Principles to Live By*

### Principle 1. God always honors our faith, but He does not promise He will always deliver us from physical death.

Shadrach, Meshach, and Abednego certainly illustrate this principle. They definitely had a strong faith. They knew beyond a shadow of a doubt that the Lord was "able to save" them from a fiery grave (3:17). But even if God allowed them to be consumed by the flames, they would "not worship the image of gold" (3:18).

Paul illustrates this same principle in the New Testament. Writing to the Philippians from a Roman prison, he hoped to be set free to continue his ministry. However, he wasn't sure what was going to happen. Consequently, he wrote that he definitely wanted Christ to "be exalted" in his "body, whether by life or by death" (Phil. 1:20).

Many other New Testament Christians died because they refused to renounce their faith in Jesus Christ. We read that "they were stoned; they were sawed in two; they were put to death by the sword" (Heb. 11:37). Some lived in spite of severe persecution, but all of them were "commended for their faith" (11:39).

As a senior pastor, I often have the privilege of praying for sick people along with a group of godly men who serve with me as elders at Fellowship Bible Church North. We take seriously James's exhortation to sick people to feel free to "call the elders of the church to pray" for them (James 5:14). Even though we pray in faith for physical restoration, we are aware that God has never promised to always heal and deliver that person from sickness. If that were true, some people would never die. However, this does not diminish our faith. We recognize that God is a sovereign God who makes the ultimate decisions about life and death. Sometimes He responds to our specific prayers and heals—sometimes completely and sometimes partially. At other times, He responds to our prayers by giving sustaining grace to live with the illness—just as He provided grace for Paul when He responded to the apostle's prayer for healing: "My grace is sufficient for you, for my power is made perfect in weakness" (2 Cor. 12:9). God has also answered our prayers by providing grace to enable the sick person we've prayed for to face death triumphantly.

*Principle 2. No matter what the outcome, as Christians we should never compromise our faith by worshiping false gods.* This was also part of Paul's prayer when he faced the prospect of death in prison. Again, writing to the Philippians, he expressed his certainty "that through" their "prayers and the help given by the Spirit of Jesus Christ," what had happened would "turn out for" his "deliverance." However, the "deliverance" Paul was sure of was not release from prison, but that he would never be ashamed to exalt Jesus Christ whether he lived or died (Phil. 2:19–20).

In this instance, "deliverance" for Paul meant taking a stand for Jesus Christ. On a previous occasion, Paul had written to the Roman Christians that he was "not ashamed of the gospel" (Rom. 1:16). Now that he was in Rome ready to face possible death, these words were doubtless ringing in his ears. In fact, his critics, who had probably read or had at least heard about his bold statement in his Roman letter, may have let Paul know they believed he would fail to practice what he preached when he faced his death.

Paul's confident response reminds us once again of Polycarp's experience. Given the opportunity several times to recant, he never compromised his faith by worshiping a false god—in this case, the Roman emperor. He faced death triumphantly, knowing that he would be "delivered" from this world to meet Jesus Christ face to face.

*Principle 3. When a Christian is threatened with physical death, he will always be delivered—either to live life on this earth or to experience total freedom in the life to come.*

After Paul wrote his letter to the Philippians, he was literally "delivered" from prison and probably had the opportunity to once again minister to these Christians. However, the time came in his life when he was not delivered from a martyr's death, but he was "delivered" from his body—the house he lived in on this earth—to be in the presence of Jesus Christ. When imprisoned the second time in Rome, Paul knew he was going to die when he wrote his second letter to Timothy. This was also the last letter he wrote. "For I am already being poured out like a drink offering," he wrote, "and the time has come for my departure" (2 Tim. 4:6). Here Paul was not talking about his departure from prison to be free once again. Rather, he was talking about his departure to be with Christ. Thus he continued: "I have fought the good fight, I have finished the race, I have kept the faith. Now there is in store for me the crown of righteousness, which the Lord, the righteous Judge, will award to me on that day—and not only to me, but also to all who have longed for his appearing" (2 Tim. 4:7–8).

Paul's death reminds me of a missionary couple named John and Betty Stam. Missionaries to China, they were taken captive by communist bandits on December 7, 1934. These ruthless men demanded a $20,000 ransom, but before anyone could negotiate a settlement, the missionaries were left dead beside the road. Their heads were literally severed from their bodies.

When news of this tragedy reached Moody Bible Institute in Chicago, the school where they had prepared for the mission field, Dr. Will Houghton, who was president, wrote a poem in their honor entitled "By Life or by Death." Inspired by both Paul's words to the Philippians and the death of this faithful couple, he penned these powerful and beautiful words:

> *So this is life, this world with all its pleasures,*
> *Struggles and tears, a smile, a frown, a sigh,*
> *Friendship so true, and love of kin and neighbor,*
> *Sometimes 'tis hard to live—always, to die!*
> *The world moves on, so rapidly the living*
> *The forms of those who disappear replace,*
> *And each one dreams that he will be enduring—*
> *How soon that one becomes the missing face!*
>
> *In life or death—and life is surely flying,*
> *The crib and coffin carved from the self-same tree.*
> *In life or death—and death so soon is coming—*
> *Escape I cannot, there's no place to flee—*
> *But Thou, O God, hast life that is eternal;*
> *That life is mine, a gift through Thy dear Son,*
> *Help me to feel its flush and pulse supernal,*
> *Assurance of the morn when life is done.*
> *Help me to know the value of these hours,*
> *Help me the folly of all waste to see;*
> *Help me to trust the Christ who bore my sorrows,*
> *And thus to yield for life or death to Thee.*
> *In all my ways be glorified, Lord Jesus,*
> *In all my ways guide me with Thine own eye;*
> *Just when and as Thou wilt, use me, Lord Jesus,*
> *And then for me 'tis Christ, to live or die.*[2]

## Personalizing These Principles

Most of us may never face the kind of persecution faced by Shadrach, Meshach, and Abednego, by the apostle Paul, and by John and Betty Stam. However, we will face decisive moments in our lives when we have to make tough choices to never compromise our faith in Jesus Christ. Use the following questions to evaluate your own life:

1. What price are you willing to pay to avoid compromising your faith?

2. What choices have you made recently in order to avoid worshiping "false gods"?

3. What "false gods" are there that you have chosen to reject? Can you list some "false gods" you've "bowed down to" but that you should reject immediately?

*Set a Goal*

As you've evaluated your own life, has the Holy Spirit revealed any "false gods" you need to reject? If so, set a personal goal to follow the example of Shadrach, Meshach, and Abednego:

_____

_____

_____

*Memorize the Following Scripture*

> *You shall have no other gods before me. You shall not make for yourself an idol in the form of anything in heaven above or on the earth beneath or in the waters below. You shall not bow down to them or worship them; for I, the Lord your God, am a jealous God.*
>
> Exodus 20:3–5a

*Growing Together*

1. What kind of "false gods" are there in this world that are capturing the affections of even Christians?

2. How can we avoid worshiping these "false gods"?

3. What "false gods" are you being tempted to worship?

4. How can we avoid yielding to this kind of temptation?

5. What can we pray for you specifically?

# Chapter 6

# *The Price of Pride*
### Read Daniel 4:1–37

*S*uppose I told you Saddam Hussein posted a story on the Internet in which he related a very personal experience. For seven years, he lost his mind and lived in the Middle Eastern desert subsisting on wild plants and grass. At nights he slept in the open air, and in the evening his body was drenched with dew. His shaggy hair grew until it reached his waist, and his fingernails looked like eagles' claws. In essence, he lived like an animal, unable to think or reason like a human being.

And then one day, Hussein came to his senses. His mind was restored. He bathed, clothed himself, cut his hair, and trimmed his nails. He then returned to Baghdad and once again became king of Iraq. However, he was a *different* man. He acknowledged for the whole world to hear that the "gods" he had worshiped—power, sensuality, and money—were all false and a reflection of his own arrogance. He even explained that his view of Allah was a distorted and false view of deity. He proclaimed that he now worshiped the one true God—the God of the Bible, the God of his own father Abraham.

His final words were gripping. He admitted his pride and proclaimed: "Now I, Saddam Hussein, praise and exalt and glorify the King of heaven, because everything he does is right and all his ways are just. And those who walk in pride he is able to humble" (Dan. 4:37, adapted).

Obviously this story is not true. It would be exciting if it were. However, this is exactly what happened to

Nebuchadnezzar, the king of Babylon—the man who is Saddam Hussein's hero and who reigned centuries before and ruled over a territory that included modern Iraq. God humbled this great king and royal ruler.[1]

## An Arrogant Attitude (4:29–32)

It all happened one day while Nebuchadnezzar "was walking on the roof" of his "royal palace" in Babylon. Reflecting on his impressive accomplishments, he said, "'Is not this the great Babylon I have built as the royal residence, by my mighty power and for the glory of my majesty?'" (Dan. 4:30).

At that moment, God responded to this arrogant statement, informing Nebuchadnezzar that He was removing his authority. He would lose his mind and for seven years he would live like an animal—until he acknowledged that "the Most High is sovereign over the kingdoms of men and gives them to anyone he wishes" (4:32).

## A Powerful Tribute (4:1–3)

This chapter in Daniel is a detailed first-person account of what happened to King Nebuchadnezzar. He was reflecting back on his incredible experience. But before he told his story, he began with a greeting to the world of his day, followed by a personal witness regarding the eternal God. "'It is my pleasure,'" he wrote, "'to tell you about the miraculous signs and wonders that the Most High God has performed for me.'" Continuing, he proclaimed: "'How great are his signs, How mighty his wonders! His kingdom is an eternal kingdom; His dominion endures from generation to generation'" (Dan. 4:3).

## Another Troublesome Dream (4:4–5)

It all began with another dream—approximately thirty years after Nebuchadnezzar's first dream (2:1–35). Daniel, no longer a teenager, was probably between forty-five and fifty years old. During the same period of time, Nebuchadnezzar had ruled Babylon between thirty and thirty-five years. He had conquered many nations and his kingdom had become one of the most powerful in the world.

One day the king was relaxing in his elegant palace. He was "contented," feeling he had reached his lifetime goal—to be the greatest monarch who ever lived. No doubt enjoying the elegance and opulence that pervaded his personal residence, he was filled with pride and self-satisfaction (4:4).

## The Wise Men's Failure (4:6–7)

That very night, Nebuchadnezzar had a terrifying dream (4:5). The emotional tranquillity that he had just experienced evaporated and he was gripped with fear. Immediately he called for all of the wise men in Babylon to gather around him and to interpret the dream. Unlike his response years earlier, he played no games. He did not test them by commanding them to both tell him the details of the dream and then to interpret it (2:3–6). Rather, he explained up front what he had seen and asked them to give him the meaning. Though the NIV text reads that "they *could not* interpret" the dream, the Hebrew text makes it clear that "they *did not*" interpret it. In other words, they didn't even attempt to use their magical books and formulas.

"Why?" you ask. These so-called "wise men" were no doubt filled with intense fear. As we'll see, even an amateur psychologist could speculate as to the meaning of the dream. But if they had, it could easily send the king into a terrible rage. After all, many of these men had served Nebuchadnezzar for years, and they knew what had happened on other occasions when he got angry and irrational. Though years had passed, no one would have forgotten his first dream and his terrible threats to "cut" them "into pieces" and to level their homes (2:5–6). And who would ever forget the "fiery furnace" experience when Shadrach, Meshach, and Abednego refused to bow down to the huge image the king had erected in the desert (3:1–30)?

## *Daniel's Sudden Appearance (4:8–9)*

Daniel, who had ruled at Nebuchadnezzar's side as a faithful servant, suddenly appeared—but only after no other wise men would comment on what the dream meant. In fact, Daniel obviously waited until just the right moment.

The word *finally* is significant in the biblical text (4:8). Daniel not only waited for the right moment, but he waited until all of the other "magicians, enchanters, astrologers, and diviners" had failed—or even refused to try to interpret the dream. Daniel knew this was another divine moment orchestrated by God to help King Nebuchadnezzar come to grips with his arrogance and false beliefs. Being sensitive to God's Spirit, Daniel entered the king's presence, knowing he would encounter an open heart and mind.

Nebuchadnezzar was elated to see Daniel. Identifying him with his Babylonian name, Belteshazzar, he also acknowledged Daniel's divine wisdom and spiritual reputation. Obviously, he had not forgotten what Daniel had done years before in both revealing his dream and interpreting it (4:9; 2:24–45). The king wasted no time explaining what had happened.

## *The Dream Details (4:10–18)*

The details of this dream moved from the inanimate to the animate—from plant life to animal life. More specifically, the first part of the dream involved a gigantic tree that was eventually cut down, leaving only a stump but roots that didn't die. The second part of the dream takes on human life. The "tree" suddenly becomes a "man."

With this in mind, note carefully the specific content of this strange dream:

### Part I: A Gigantic Tree

> *I looked, and there before me stood a tree in the middle of the land. Its height was enormous. The tree grew large and strong and*

*its top touched the sky; it was visible to the ends of the earth. Its leaves were beautiful, its fruit abundant, and on it was food for all. Under it the beasts of the field found shelter, and the birds of the air lived in its branches; from it every creature was fed.*

*In the visions I saw while lying in my bed, I looked, and there before me was a messenger, a holy one, coming down from heaven. He called in a loud voice: "cut down the tree and trim off its branches; strip off its leaves and scatter its fruit. Let the animals flee from under it and the birds from its branches. But let the stump and its roots, bound with iron and bronze, remain in the ground, in the grass of the field" (4:10b–15a).*

## Part II: The Tree Is a Man

*Let him be drenched with the dew of heaven, and let him live with the animals among the plants of the earth. Let his mind be changed from that of a man and let him be given the mind of an animal, till seven times pass by for him.*

*The decision is announced by messengers, the holy ones declare the verdict, so that the living may know that the Most High is sovereign over the kingdoms of men and gives them to anyone he wishes and sets over them the lowliest of men (4:15b–17).*

## *Daniel's Interpretation (4:19–26)*

Though the biblical record reads that Daniel "was greatly perplexed for a time," it does not mean that he was confused regarding the meaning of the dream. Rather, he was "afraid for the king." In fact, Daniel's "thoughts terrified him." His emotions were so obvious that the king attempted to comfort Daniel—to put him at ease. "Do not let the dream or its meaning alarm you," Nebuchadnezzar advised (4:19).

Daniel finally became courageous enough to relay the meaning of the dream. However, he let the king know up front that he wished he could give a different interpretation—

one that was more like the meaning of the dream he had interpreted years before. At that time, Nebuchadnezzar was the "head of gold" (2:38)— "the king of kings" (2:37). God had given him "dominion and power and might and glory" (2:37). The Lord had "placed mankind and the beasts of the field and the birds of the air" in his hands (2:38).

However, the content of this present dream stood out in stark contrast. This meaning didn't even apply to Nebuchadnezzar's "enemies" and "adversaries"—even though Daniel wished it had (4:19). Furthermore, the messenger who issued the order to "cut down the tree and destroy it" came from the one true God—"the Most High" (4:24). Nebuchadnezzar would "be driven away" from his people to "live with the wild animals." He would "eat grass like cattle and be drenched with the dew of heaven." He would actually live like an animal for seven years until he acknowledged that God, the Most High, is sovereign over the kingdoms of men and gives them to anyone He wishes (4:24–25).

There was, however, one positive element in the dream. Though there would only be a stump left in the ground, its roots would not die. Just so, Nebuchadnezzar would be restored to his kingship once he acknowledged the one true God as the ruler of the universe (4:26).

## *A Period of Grace (4:27–30)*

Daniel then hastened to advise the king that God "might change His mind" as He had done so many times before in biblical history. Daniel's exhortation was direct, straightforward, and specific: "Renounce your sins by doing what is right, and your wickedness by being kind to the oppressed. It may be that then your prosperity will continue" (4:27).

Unfortunately, Nebuchadnezzar did not heed Daniel's advice. He continued to relish his luxury and splendor and to take credit for what he had accomplished. His comments were boastful and filled with arrogance: "'Is not this the great Babylon I have built as a royal residence, by my mighty power and for the glory of my majesty?'" (4:30).

Another year went by and God patiently waited, giving Nebuchadnezzar time to repent (4:29). Sadly, the king took advantage of God's grace and continued to harden his heart. Then it happened just as Daniel predicted (4:28–33). God's judgment fell on this arrogant monarch.

## Seven Painful Years (4:31–33)

Because Nebuchadnezzar failed to heed Daniel's plea to humble himself, this powerful ruler lost his "royal authority." All that Daniel predicted happened, once again verifying his prophetic gift. In fact, the prophecy was confirmed by "a voice" that came directly from God Himself (4:31).

Imagine the scene! This man who at one time was dressed in elegant robes and wore a kingly crown was down on all fours eating grass with the cattle of the field. This bizarre behavior continued for seven years and during this time, "his hair grew like the feathers of an eagle and his nails like the claws of a bird" (4:33). What an incredible scene! This mighty "head of gold" became a "stump of a tree."

## A Miraculous Restoration (4:34–36)

Though Nebuchadnezzar was irrational during this seven years of horrible judgment, he was still able to turn his "eyes toward heaven," to repent from his arrogance, and to acknowledge God (4:34). In other words, the Lord had not totally removed His grace from Nebuchadnezzar. Once this pathetic creature took one faltering step toward the Lord, he experienced redemption. God restored Nebuchadnezzar's sanity, enabling this once proud king to respond with worship and praise.

Again, imagine the scene. This once proud monarch fell on his knees. Though naked and filthy, with matted hair and fingernails that were gnarled and jagged, Nebuchadnezzar lifted his voice to the eternal God and cried out:

> *His dominion is an eternal dominion;*
>> *his kingdom endures from generation to generation.*
> *All the peoples of the earth*
>> *are regarded as nothing.*
> *He does as he pleases*
>> *with the powers of heaven*
>> *and the peoples of the earth.*
> *No one can hold back his hand*
>> *or say to him: "What have you done?" (4:34–35).*

We are not told specifically what happened following Nebuchadnezzar's repentance except that he returned to the city of Babylon. Perhaps he sought out Daniel, his trusted friend and fellow magistrate—who had no doubt continued to serve as ruler during his absence. We do know that once he returned, his "advisors and nobles sought" him out and he "was restored" to his "throne," and Nebuchadnezzar became even greater than before (4:36).

## A Final Tribute (4:37)

When Nebuchadnezzar once again occupied his throne, he was a different man. Some believe his restoration was also his moment of conversion, when he passed from eternal death into eternal life. Though it may have taken him time to renounce all of his pagan gods, he clearly acknowledged his faith in the God of Abraham, Isaac, and Jacob. His personal testimony is clear and unequivocal: *"Now I, Nebuchadnezzar, praise and exalt and glorify the King of heaven, because everything he does is right and all his ways are just"* (4:37).

Nebuchadnezzar also learned one of the greatest lessons any man can learn—that God honors those who are truly humble, "and those who walk in pride he is able to humble"

(4:37b). For any person Christian or non-Christian to ignore this great truth is to risk everything we have on this earth— our vocations, our families, and our personal well-being. Ultimately, we will pay a horrible price for arrogance.

## Becoming God's Man Today

*Principles to Live By*

### Principle 1. God seriously disapproves of pride and arrogance.

This is the primary lesson we can learn from this dramatic event in Nebuchadnezzar's life. He was a proud, arrogant man. He took credit for everything he did and had.

God's attitude toward pride is clear throughout the Bible, but no scriptural statement is more vivid and unequivocal than what we read in Proverbs:

> *There are six things the Lord hates,*
> *seven that are detestable to him:*
> > *haughty eyes,*
> > *a lying tongue,*
> > *hands that shed innocent blood,*
> > *a heart that devises wicked schemes,*
> > *feet that are quick to rush into evil,*
> > *a false witness who pours out lies*
> > *and a man who stirs up dissension among*
> > *brothers (Prov. 6:16–19).*

### A Reflection of Satan

It's not accidental that "pride" stands at the top of the list of terrible sins. Here it is described as having "haughty eyes." What others see in our eyes are "reflections of the soul," and this kind of reflection has its roots in Satan himself. It was his downfall when he was called Lucifer—the morning star—the principal angel (Isa. 14:12). Isaiah recorded that he made five very arrogant statements in the presence of the sovereign God:

- "I will ascend to heaven."
- "I will raise my throne above the stars of God."
- "I will sit enthroned on the mount of assembly, on the utmost heights of the sacred mountain."
- "I will ascend above the tops of the clouds."
- "I will make myself like the Most High" (14:13–14).

As a result of Satan's prideful actions, he was "cast down to the earth" (14:12). He lost his position in heaven. Ever since then, he and a host of demons who followed him have targeted all human beings, attempting to trap them in the same sin.

Satan himself even tried this tactic on Jesus Christ when he tempted Him in the wilderness. Matthew recorded that "the devil took him to a very high mountain and showed him all the kingdoms of the world and their splendor." Satan then promised Jesus that he would give Him all of this if He would "bow down and worship." Jesus' response is a wonderful example to us all. He said, "Away from me, Satan! For it is written: 'Worship the Lord your God, and serve him only'" (Matt. 4:8–10).

## A Reflection of Jesus Christ

Jesus Christ demonstrated this quality of humility throughout His life. The apostle Paul appealed to His example when he wrote to the Philippians and said, "Do nothing out of selfish ambition or vain conceit, but in humility consider others better than yourselves. Each of you should look not only to your own interests, but also to the interests of others" (Phil. 2:3–4).

Paul then made it clear that Jesus Christ was indeed our supreme example:

> *"Your attitude should be the same as that of Christ Jesus: who, being in the very nature of God, did not consider equality with God something to be grasped, but **made himself nothing**, taking*

*the very nature of a servant, being made in human likeness. And being found in appearance as a man, **he humbled himself** and became obedient to death—even death on a cross!" (Phil. 2:5–8).*

### *Principle 2. Though God "hates" pride, He is patient and wants us to turn from this sin so that He will not have to discipline us.*

As prideful as Nebuchadnezzar was, God gave him a full year to repent after warning him about his coming downfall. Daniel also made it clear that God might respond to a humble spirit and not bring this judgment on Nebuchadnezzar. Sadly, the king didn't listen and suffered the consequences.

God continues to extend His grace to both Christians and non-Christians—even when we have the Word of God that tells us that pride comes before a fall (Prov. 29:23; 1 Cor. 10:12). However, He will not tolerate this kind of behavior indefinitely. Eventually, God will humble us!

As Christians, we must take God's Word seriously. Just because we are successful and even contented doesn't mean that God will not eventually deal with our sin. Since we are God's children and He is a loving Father, He will discipline us in due time in order to help us conform our lives to His will (Heb. 12:7–10).

If we are not true Christians, God will extend His grace so that we can come to know Him personally—giving us the opportunity to acknowledge our sins and to receive the Lord Jesus Christ as our personal Savior. However, as with Nebuchadnezzar, He may allow us eventually to self-destruct in order to come to the place in our lives where we know that we need God.

### *Principle 3. God will respond to our prayers for help when we acknowledge our sins and seek His help.*

This principle applies to both Christians and non-Christians. For true believers, God is waiting and longing for us to be back in fellowship with Him. He will never turn His back on us. However, the Lord is fully aware of our motives. He knows when we are playing games with Him. He sees our hearts, and because of His love, He will not allow us to manipulate Him. He will keep the pressure on until He sees the sincerity of our hearts and that we are truly repentant.

The encouraging aspect of this story for people who are not true believers is that the moment Nebuchadnezzar lifted his eyes to the Lord, even in his demented state, God responded. As Peter reminds us, the Lord "is patient" with us, "not wanting anyone to perish, but everyone to come to repentance" (1 Peter 3:9).

If you are not sure you are a Christian, will you humble yourself before Him today, confess your sin of pride (which we all have), and receive the Lord Jesus Christ as your personal Savior from sin? "For God so loved the world that he gave his one and only Son, that whoever believes in him shall not perish but have eternal life" (John 3:16).

## Personalizing These Principles

The following questions will help you search your own heart regarding the way you are applying these principles:

1. To what extent have you allowed pride to control your life? Are you reflecting Satan's character or the character of Jesus Christ?

2. To what extent are you taking advantage of God's grace? Are you interpreting the positive events in your life as God's blessing in spite of your sin?

3. Has Satan deceived you, causing you to think you are too sinful for God to respond to your prayers for help?

Remember, it is never too late to return to God! The thief who deserved to die for his criminal activities cried out to

Jesus Christ as they hung on their separate crosses. Jesus responded with these wonderful words: "I tell you the truth, today you will be with me in paradise" (Luke 23:43).

## Set a Goal

How has the Holy Spirit spoken to your heart as you've reflected on these divine principles? Set at least one goal for your life and ask the Lord to help you achieve it:

_____

_____

_____

_____

## Memorize the Following Scripture

*For whoever exalts himself will be humbled, and whoever humbles himself will be exalted.*
Matthew 23:12

## Growing Together

1. Why is it so easy to allow pride to control our lives, even as Christians?

2. How can we recognize pride in our lives—including "false humility"?

3. Would you feel free to share some of these areas in your own life where you struggle with this tendency and how you deal with this temptation?

4. What can we pray for you specifically?

# Chapter 7

# A Disastrous Party

Read Daniel 5:1–31

*A*t this point in Babylonian history, the empire was in serious trouble. Over thirty years had passed since King Nebuchadnezzar's period of insanity. Daniel was now more than eighty years old and was virtually forgotten by Babylonian royal leaders. Cyrus' Persian forces had captured every major post—except the city of Babylon.

Belshazzar, who served as co-regent with his absentee father, Nabonidus, was in charge of the city. He deceived himself into thinking Babylon was impregnable—and with some good reasons. The city was surrounded with a gigantic double wall over thirty feet high that contained more than one hundred strategically placed towers. The Euphrates River ran under the wall and through the city, guaranteeing a constant supply of water. Furthermore, Belshazzar had stockpiled enough food within the walls to last for twenty years.

However, not everyone within the city walls felt secure. The Persian army had surrounded Babylon. The men assigned to man the towers had certainly reported every military maneuver, which would have created nervous conversations among the city's inhabitants—from street vendors to those who made up the royal family.

## A Great Banquet (5:1–4)

Have you ever felt insecure and tried to prove yourself with self-centered behavior? In other words, you've tried to make yourself look good to overcome your fear and anxiety. This may have been one reason why Belshazzar planned this "great banquet." However, he was no doubt also concerned about the insecurity people were feeling within the city walls. He certainly wanted to reassure everyone that he was in control and they had nothing to fear. What better way to put people at ease than to invite all of his leading men, "a thousand of his nobles," to "a great banquet" that allowed them to eat, drink, and be merry (5:1)? Belshazzar took the lead—probably sitting at his own private table—and was the first to begin to drink their vintage wine.

## A Drunken Orgy

However, this pagan banquet was far more than a drinking party for a group of royal men. Belshazzar invited all of his wives and concubines—which probably at least equaled the thousand nobles. Before long, this huge dinner party turned into a drunken orgy—with King Belshazzar setting the pace.

In the midst of this pagan revelry, Belshazzar did something that no Babylonian king had ever done. While imbibing his wine—and obviously losing any sense of decency—"he gave orders to bring in the gold and silver goblets that Nebuchadnezzar his father [grandfather] had taken from the temple in Jerusalem" (5:2).[1]

This reference to Nebuchadnezzar takes us back nearly sixty-five years when Daniel was taken captive and brought to Babylon, along with the sacred articles from the "temple of God" in Jerusalem (1:2). Even though these items were placed in the pagan temple in Babylon, "protocol" dictated that golden and silver goblets were never to be removed from the "treasure house" of the Babylonian gods and used to honor the king himself.

## An Act of Rebellion

Belshazzar's decision to stage this banquet was also a deliberate act of rebellion against the God of Abraham, Isaac, and Jacob. While he and "his nobles, his wives and his concubines drank" from these sacred vessels, he had everyone praise the

Babylonian "gods of gold and silver, of bronze, iron, wood and stone" (5:4). Obviously, Belshazzar was attempting to eliminate any glory and honor that his grandfather Nebuchadnezzar had given to the one true God! Incidentally, the fact that there were enough "gold goblets" (5:3), excluding the "silver goblets" (5:2), to serve at least two thousand people, gives us an idea of the number and value of the sacred "articles" Nebuchadnezzar removed from the temple in Jerusalem and carried back to Babylon. It also gives us a glimpse into Belshazzar's mental state when he ordered both sets of goblets. He was no doubt already out of touch with reality.[2]

## The Fingers of a Human Hand (5:5–9)

King Belshazzar was in for the surprise of his life. While he and his nobles were engaging in unspeakable idolatry and immorality, "the fingers of a human hand appeared and wrote on the plaster of the wall" (5:5). The king was definitely sober enough to see what was happening. He actually "watched the hand as it wrote."

### A Sobering Event

Though Belshazzar had lost his ability to think clearly because of his intake of alcohol, he was suddenly jarred out of this state—at least sufficiently to be able to comprehend what was happening. Crises have a way of sobering people up!

I remember one Christmas evening my family and I were driving up a winding road to Crested Butte Mountain in Colorado. It had been snowing most of the day, and it was still coming down at least an inch an hour. Suddenly, we all looked up and saw a car's headlights ahead of us. What the driver didn't realize while driving at a dangerous speed was that he was rapidly headed for a 90-degree curve in the road. We all held our breath as we watched this car cross in front of us and then slam into a ditch. As he came to a sudden stop, the impact was so great that the rear end of the car came straight up. All of this happened about ten feet in front of us. The car rose as if in slow motion, stood on its front end for a moment, and then turned in midair and fell back on its wheels.

Startled and concerned, I quickly ran to the damaged car and opened the door. The driver was definitely confused, but remarkably alert, even though he was drunk. He suddenly realized he had totally miscalculated his speed, the terrain, and his ability to think and drive a car. It's amazing what a crisis can do to snap a person out of a drunken state!

## A Frightening Experience

When King Belshazzar saw what was happening, the blood drained from his face. He also sobered up. He literally "turned pale." We read that "he was so frightened that his knees knocked" and literally buckled under him (5:6).

The words printed on the wall, though written with the Babylonian alphabet, were unintelligible to the king. Consequently, he called for all of his wise men—"enchanters, astrologers and diviners"—and told them that any one of them who could read what was written and explain the meaning would be greatly rewarded. He promised to clothe that person "in purple." Furthermore, he would "have a gold chain placed around his neck." And to top it off, Belshazzar announced that he would elevate that person to "the third highest ruler in the kingdom" (5:7). This final promise substantiates secular history, namely that Belshazzar and his father, Nabonidus, were co-regents. In other words, any man who would read what was written and interpret the meaning would be a part of a triumvirate and on the same level as Belshazzar and his father.[3]

In spite of this incredible offer, not one of the wise men could read or interpret the writing. They had no clue—which only added to Belshazzar's intense fear. In fact, he "became even more terrified and his face grew more pale" (5:9).

You can imagine what was happening among those who had been invited to the banquet. Needless to say, they were "baffled"

(5:9), a word translated from an original word meaning "greatly perplexed" and reflecting animated confusion. In other words, the one thousand nobles were suddenly running about the room, shouting and gesturing wildly. What could this mean, especially in view of the fact that the Persian army had surrounded the city? Even though their minds had been numbed with alcohol, they realized this could be a terribly bad omen.

## *"Call for Daniel" (5:10–12)*

Word spread rapidly throughout the palace regarding this dramatic and frightening event. In fact, the king and his nobles were shouting so loudly that the queen herself "came into the banquet hall" (5:10).

Who was this "queen"? Evidently, it was Belshazzar's mother—the wife of his father Nabonidus and Nebuchadnezzar's daughter. In other words, she was the "Queen Mother." This explains why she knew about Daniel. She had lived during the time he had interpreted her father's dreams—particularly the one that predicted Nebuchadnezzar's period of insanity (4:24–26).

When Nitocris (the queen's name is identified in secular history) arrived on the scene, she quickly assessed the situation and took control. She told Belshazzar that Daniel was still alive—a man his grandfather Nebuchadnezzar had appointed as "chief of the magicians, enchanters, astrologers and diviners" (5:11). She was also quick to review Daniel's qualifications—a wise man who had "a keen mind and knowledge and understanding, and also the ability to interpret dreams, explain riddles and solve difficult problems" (5:12). Without wavering regarding this old man's supernatural abilities (5:11), she told Belshazzar to "call for Daniel." She was absolutely confident that he could unravel the meaning of the words and explain any secret message—which indicates how well she knew him. Some believe she may have been a true believer in the one true God.

## "Are You Daniel?" (5:13–16)

Belshazzar wasted no time following his mother's instructions, which indicates his state of panic. This was no time to revert to adolescent behavior. He ordered Daniel to appear before him and came directly to the point when this old sage entered the banquet hall. Interestingly, Belshazzar's statements reveal that he may have known more about Daniel than the queen mother thought. Though the king had probably never interfaced with Daniel, he certainly had heard dramatic stories about his wisdom. Could it be that Belshazzar had been threatened by what he had heard and consequently had tried to ignore Daniel? Could this be why he had also ordered the sacred goblets that had been taken from the temple in Jerusalem to be used to praise their gods rather than Daniel's God?

Whatever the reasons as to why Belshazzar had not sought Daniel out earlier, he knew he had no choice at this moment but to pay tribute to this old prophet's supernatural wisdom and abilities (5:14). He quickly acknowledged that his own wise men had failed (5:15). He then promised Daniel the same rewards if he could read the writing and interpret the meaning (5:16).

## "You Knew All This!" (5:17–21)

Daniel had probably been praying for this moment—this unique opportunity to bear witness for the Lord God—and his response must have surprised the king. "You may keep your gifts for yourself and give your rewards to someone else," Daniel responded. "Nevertheless, I will read the writing for the king and tell him what it means" (5:17). In other words, Daniel wanted Belshazzar to know up front that he wasn't motivated by material possessions, earthly prestige, and kingly power.

Before Daniel read the writing on the wall and interpreted the meaning, he conveyed a very pointed message to Belshazzar. He reviewed for the king what had happened to Nebuchadnezzar, making it clear that this man's "sovereignty and greatness and glory and splendor" came from "the Most High God" (5:18). But Daniel also reminded Belshazzar that his grandfather had used his high position selfishly and had become arrogant. He had used his power to hurt people and to bring honor to himself. Consequently, "he was deposed from his royal throne and stripped of his glory" (5:20). He went insane and lived like an animal—"until he acknowledged that the Most High God is sovereign over the kingdom of men and sets over them anyone he wishes" (5:21).

## *"You . . . Have Not Humbled Yourself" (5:22–24)*

At this point, Daniel gives us a very helpful insight. What he had just shared with Belshazzar was nothing new to this man. The king had known very specifically what had happened to his grandfather and why it happened (5:22). In spite of this specific knowledge, Daniel chided Belshazzar for not humbling himself and learning from the lesson God taught his grandfather. Daniel's explanation underscores our earlier conclusion that Belshazzar had deliberately set out to show disrespect and dishonor to the Lord God that his grandfather Nebuchadnezzar had both acknowledged and worshiped. Daniel's exhortation speaks for itself: "But you his son, O Belshazzar, have not humbled yourself, though you knew all this. Instead, you have set yourself up against the Lord of heaven. You had the goblets from his temple brought to you, and you and your nobles, your wives and your concubines drank wine from them. You praised the gods of silver and gold, of bronze, iron, wood and stone, which cannot see or hear or understand. But you did not honor the God who holds in his hand your life and all your ways" (5:22–23).

## *"You Have Been Found Wanting" (5:25–30)*

Following this indictment, Daniel proceeded to read the inscription: "mene, mene, tekel, parsin" (5:25).

Daniel then explained what these words meant.

- "*Mene:* God has numbered the days of your reign and brought it to an end" (5:26).

   The first word, *Mene,* meant that Belshazzar's days as king had come to an end. His time to humble himself and acknowledge the one true God had run out. It was all over! No matter what he tried to do, nothing could change the course of history for Belshazzar.

- "*Tekel:* You have been weighed on the scales and found wanting" (5:27).

   With the word *Tekel,* the Lord used a metaphor to demonstrate to Belshazzar—and to all his nobles—that the king had not responded to the light God had given him, even though he knew everything that had happened to his grandfather Nebuchadnezzar—and why it happened. He continued in his arrogance and proceeded to even desecrate the "goblets of gold" that were originally created to worship Jehovah God. He had sealed his own doom.

- "*Peres:* Your kingdom is divided and given to the Medes and Persians" (5:28).

   The word *Peres* is the singular of the word *Parsin.* The word in itself meant "divided" and the meaning is clear from both prophecy and history. "That very night Belshazzar, king of the Babylonians, was slain, and Darius the Mede took over the kingdom, at the age of sixty-two" (5:30–31).

After Belshazzar understood the words and their meaning, he immediately clothed Daniel in purple and placed a gold chain around his neck. He then proclaimed that this old prophet was "the third highest ruler in the kingdom" (5:29).

Was this Belshazzar's effort at appeasing God—to stay his hand of execution? Possibly. If so, it didn't work! The facts are, he took the wrong approach. He honored Daniel, not Daniel's God. There is no evidence that he humbled himself before the Lord.

But this raises another question. If Belshazzar had clothed himself in sackcloth and ashes and truly repented, would God have preserved his life? We cannot answer this question specifically except to say that in the Old Testament, God always demonstrated mercy when there was true repentance. The facts are that Belshazzar did not repent—and suffered the consequences—which leads to the rest of God's message of doom.

At this point, secular history once again helps us understand what actually happened. The Persian army diverted the Euphrates River from its regular channel that went under the gigantic wall that surrounded Babylon. The water level was lowered enough so that Cyrus' soldiers then followed the riverbed right into the center of the city. Once inside, they secretly entered the great ballroom, took Belshazzar captive, and immediately took his life. Secular history also verifies that the Persian army spared the lives of Belshazzar's nobles, his wives and concubines and the rest of the people within the city. This also explains why Daniel himself survived this attack.

## Becoming God's Man Today

*Principles to Live By*

### *Principle 1. All of us have been "weighed on the scales and found wanting."*

The apostle Paul made this point very clear in his letter to the Romans. We "all have sinned and fall short of the glory of God" (Rom. 3:23). We've all missed the mark in terms of measuring up to God's perfect standard.

The Lord Jesus Christ was the exception. He was the God-man. God was His heavenly Father and Mary His earthly mother. Being without sin, He became "the lamb of God who takes away the sins of the world" (John 1:29). He sacrificed His life on the cross to pay for our sins and to provide eternal life to all who receive Him as personal Savior (John 1:12; Rom. 6:23).

This principle was true even in Old Testament times. Paraphrasing King David, Paul wrote:

> *There is no one righteous, not even one;*
> *there is no one who understands,*
> *no one who seeks God.*
> *All have turned away,*
> *they have together become worthless;*
> *there is no one who does good,*
> *not even one (Rom. 3:10–12).*

### Principle 2. All people who inherit eternal life do so by grace through faith, not by works.

Again, Paul made this clear—this time in his letter to the Ephesians: "For it is by grace you have been saved, through faith—and this not from yourselves, it is the gift of God—not by works, so that no one can boast" (Eph. 2:8–9).

It's very important to understand this principle. It may appear that God told Belshazzar He had placed his "good works" on one side of the scale and his "bad works" on the other side of the scale, and because his "bad works" outweighed his "good works," the Lord condemned him to a lost eternity, which the Bible calls hell.

Not so. No person in the Old Testament was ever saved by doing good works. No Jew, even though he followed the one true God, was saved by keeping the Ten Commandments. And no pagan who worshiped gods of wood and stone—like Belshazzar—was saved by good works. Salvation has always come through faith—and faith alone. This is why Paul made this point very clear regarding Abraham's conversion experience. After stating that we "all have sinned and fall short of the glory of God," Paul went on to explain how Abraham, a pagan idolater like Belshazzar, was saved:

> *What then shall we say that Abraham, our forefather, discovered in this matter? If, in fact, Abraham was justified by works, he had something to boast about—but not before God. What does the Scripture say? "Abraham believed God, and it was credited to him as righteousness" (Rom. 4:1–3).*

To make his point even clearer, Paul applied this principle—justification by faith—to David, who unlike Abraham, was a Jew who followed the one true God and was committed to keeping the law of God. Paul explained:

> *Now when a man works, his wages are not credited to him as a gift, but as an obligation. However, to the man who does not work but trusts God who justifies the wicked, his faith is credited as righteousness. David says the same thing when he speaks of the blessedness of the man to whom God credits righteousness apart from works:*
> *"Blessed are they*
>  *whose transgressions are forgiven,*
>  *whose sins are covered.*
> *Blessed is the man*
> *whose sin the Lord will never count against him" (Rom. 4:4–8).*

What then did God mean when He told Belshazzar he had been "weighed on the scales and found wanting"? The answer is really very simple. Belshazzar had neglected the knowledge he had received. He knew about his grandfather Nebuchadnezzar's faith in Daniel's God following his years of living like an animal. Belshazzar rejected that truth and refused to believe in the one true God like his forefather Abraham who had lived in idolatrous paganism centuries before in the very same region—Ur of the Chaldeans. God's patience had run out. As in the case of those who refused to respond to Noah's warnings for 120 years while he was building the ark, when the floods came, God shut the door (Gen. 7:11). It was too late!

*Principle 3. God continues to reach out to all people with His grace—no matter how rebellious and sinful they are.*

We also see this principle illustrated in Belshazzar's story. This is why God wrote His message of judgment on the wall of the king's banquet hall. He wanted every man and woman present to see His miraculous revelation. Though they were engaging in the worst kinds of idolatry and immorality, the Lord was warning these people not to follow Belshazzar's example. And it was not accidental that God chose this method: "the finger of a man's hand" writing on the wall! God wanted them all to see this supernatural phenomenon. He wanted all of them to understand what it meant. Furthermore, the writing remained on the wall for what had to be a long time—perhaps until the "fingers of time" removed it through a process of natural decay and deterioration.

This was God's grace to the people of Babylon. We don't know how many of those people turned from their wickedness to believe in the one true God and to experience salvation. However, I personally believe I'll someday meet some of these people in heaven.

And don't forget that God kept the Persian army from destroying these people. As far as we know, the only one who died at the hands of Darius the Mede was Belshazzar. As God has done periodically, He brought judgment "on a few" to reach "the many." Ananias and Sapphira illustrate this point in the New Testament. They intentionally and flagrantly lied to the Holy Spirit and dropped dead (Acts 5:1–10). But note the result: "Great fear seized the whole church and all who heard about these events" (Acts 5:11). Imagine the fear that must have gripped Belshazzar's nobles and his wives and concubines following Daniel's "sermon" and his interpretation of the "handwriting on the wall"—which was followed by Belshazzar's assassination! Hopefully, many of these people put their faith in the God of Abraham, Isaac, and Jacob.

*Principle 4. God's patience with sinful humanity is definitely correlated with the way we respond to what we know about His will for our lives.*

Daniel made this point very clear to Belshazzar. This is the true meaning behind the word Tekel—to be weighed on a scale and found wanting. "You knew all this," Daniel said, [and yet] "you have not humbled yourself" (Dan. 5:22). Furthermore, Belshazzar deliberately "got in God's face" and used the "golden goblets" from the temple in Jerusalem to deny outright any faith in the Lord God. To underscore his intentions, Belshazzar used these sacred articles to worship the Babylonian gods of wood and stone.

Even then I believe God was still giving Belshazzar an opportunity to follow his grandfather Nebuchadnezzar's example—to raise his eyes toward heaven and to praise "the Most High," to honor and glorify "him who lives forever" (4:34–37). However, Belshazzar tried to manipulate God by elevating Daniel! The king definitely failed the final test and experienced both physical and eternal death.

The message is clear, particularly to people who are rejecting the gospel of Jesus Christ. In the words of the author of Hebrews, "Today, if you hear his voice, do not harden your hearts" (Heb. 3:15).

## Personalizing These Principles

The following questions and comments will help you apply these divine principles to your life. Before you proceed, ask the Lord to help you understand clearly what you are about to read:

1. Have you acknowledged that you, like all human beings, are sinful and need a Savior?

   We all fail to measure up to God's perfect standard of righteousness. If you have not told God you "have sinned and fall short of the glory of God" (Rom. 3:23), would you do that today? Simply confess to the Lord that you are a sinner and that you need salvation.

2. Do you understand that salvation is a free gift?

Not one of us can earn eternal life by doing good works. You must reach out to God by faith and receive this gift. If you haven't taken this step, invite the Lord Jesus Christ to be your Savior from sin. Remember the words of the apostle John who wrote that "to all who received him [Jesus Christ], to those who believed in his name, he gave the right to become children of God" (John 1:12).

3. Do you understand that God is still reaching out to you no matter how many sins you've committed?

Have you read about the conversation Jesus Christ had with the woman at the well in Samaria (John 4:1–41)? She had been married and divorced five times and was presently living with a man out of wedlock. When this woman heard who Jesus was, she believed in Jesus Christ, and God used her testimony to lead many others to the Savior. No matter what your moral and ethical failures, if you've confessed your sins, God "is faithful and just and will forgive us our sins and purify us from all unrighteousness" (1 John 1:9).

4. Do you understand that once people know the truth and deliberately, flagrantly, and consistently reject it, they are living dangerously?

God may simply allow us to go our own way and suffer the consequences. This is what happened to the people Paul described in Romans, chapter 1. Because they suppressed "the truth with their wickedness" (Rom. 1:18) and refused to "retain the knowledge of God" (1:28), the Lord "gave them over" to "sexual impurity" (1:24), to "shameful lusts" (1:26), and to "a depraved mind" (1:28). This is what happened to Belshazzar. This is also why the author of Hebrews warns us not to harden our hearts when we hear and understand the message of the Word of God. Now that you know these things, would you respond to God's grace in your own life? Trust in the Lord Jesus Christ today.

## Set a Goal

Ask the Holy Spirit to help you write out a goal that you want to achieve immediately:

_____

_____

_____

## Memorize the Following Scripture

*If we confess our sins, he is faithful and just and will forgive us our sins and purify us from all unrighteousness.*
1 John 1:9

## Growing Together

1. Why is it difficult for some people to acknowledge that they have sinned and need a Savior?
2. Why do people often find it difficult to understand that salvation is a free gift and that they cannot earn salvation by doing good works?
3. Why do some people come to the place in their lives where they think their sins are so great that they cannot be forgiven? How can we help these people understand that the Lord Jesus Christ paid for all sins when He died on the cross?
4. On the other hand, how can we sensitively help people understand that God allows human beings to come to a point in their lives where they create their own bondage and blindness? (Read together and discuss Romans, chapter 1.)
5. What can we pray for you personally?

Chapter 8

# An Insidious Plot
Read Daniel 6:1–28

$D$aniel's experience in the den of lions is one of the most well-known and dramatic stories in the Bible. Like every person who attended Sunday School growing up, I considered it one of my favorites. Even a child can comprehend some of the marvelous aspects of this event, especially the way God protected Daniel. Who hasn't seen an artist's rendition picturing Daniel using a lion's back for a pillow?

Unfortunately, Daniel is often pictured as a young man in this scene. In actuality, he was at least eighty-three years old—some believe older. During the Babylonian captivity, he had served three major kings—Nebuchadnezzar, Belshazzar, and now Darius—who served under Cyrus, king of Persia. In secular history, this Darius was probably a man named Gubaru. The honorific title "Darius" means "owner of the scepter" and was used to identify at least five Persian rulers. It also seems that King Darius mentioned in Daniel, chapter 6, was not "Darius the Mede" mentioned in chapter 5—who died three weeks after he captured Babylon. Cyrus, king of all Persia, had appointed Gubaru (another Darius) to serve as king over the general area that comprised the former Babylonian empire.[1]

## A New Regime (6:1–2)
The new king wasted no time rearranging the political system in Babylon and establishing a new government. In fact,

Darius was reputed to have been an administrative genius. He selected and appointed "120 satraps," or governors, to rule throughout the kingdom (6:1). The term satrap actually means "a kingdom protector."

To guarantee adequate accountability, Darius appointed "three administrators" over these 120 governors. It was their responsibility to make sure all of these men carried out their tasks in an efficient and honest manner, avoiding both waste and graft (6:2). The new government was highly centralized in terms of supervision and quite decentralized in terms of function—a reflection of the king's brilliant organizational ability.

## An Amazing Appointment (6:1–2)

From a human point of view, it's surprising that Daniel was appointed as one of these three administrators. First, he was at least eighty-three years old—an age when most leaders have retired from this kind of responsibility. This appointment indicates that Daniel was still in great health physically and mentally.

From a divine perspective, it's easy to answer this question. God was sovereignly superintending Daniel's life. Like Esther, who became queen in a foreign land, Daniel too had "come to royal position for such a time as this" (Esther 4:14).

Furthermore, Cyrus, the king of Persia, favored the Israelites. It was during the first year of his reign that he encouraged the Jews to return to Jerusalem, promising his personal help to rebuild the temple. He also ordered that all "fifty-four hundred articles of gold and silver" that Nebuchadnezzar had brought to Babylon be returned to Jerusalem (Ezra 1:1–11). This also explains why Darius who reported directly to Cyrus— would not hesitate to place a Jew in this high position.

Darius, too, was an astute leader in his own right. He certainly conducted a background check on all of these new leaders—particularly on the men who were to be his three key administrators. It wouldn't take long to discover Daniel's credentials. He had served in high positions in the Babylonian government since he was seventeen years old. His reputation as a man of wisdom was outstanding, and his character was impeccable. Though he was a foreigner, he had demonstrated incredible loyalty to his superiors and had performed his tasks admirably.

Remember too that Darius would have quickly learned what had happened at Belshazzar's feast. When all of the wise men of Babylon could not read and interpret the handwriting on the palace wall, Daniel could. And let's not forget that before Belshazzar was taken captive and executed, he had appointed Daniel as "the third highest ruler in the kingdom" (5:29). This in itself would motivate Darius to explore Daniel's background. And when he did, he discovered a man he could trust.

## Green-eyed Jealousy (6:3–5)

Whenever Daniel was given a job to do, he did it better than anyone else. This is the story of his life. In fact, in this new position he "so distinguished himself among the administrators and satraps by his exceptional qualities that the king planned to set him over the whole kingdom" (6:3).

Predictably, the other two men who had been on the same level as Daniel exploded with jealousy. They quickly spread this dreaded "emotional disease" among a number of the satraps. Together, they "tried to find grounds for charges against Daniel and his conduct of government affairs" (6:4a). However, Daniel had performed his tasks so well that these men couldn't even conjure something up that would be believable! We read that "they could find no corruption in him, because he was trustworthy and neither corrupt nor negligent" (6:4b).

## An Insidious Plot (6:5–9)

Unable to find anything wrong in the way Daniel performed his assigned duties, they decided to use his personal prayer life to build a case against him. Daniel never hesitated to practice his beliefs in public. "Three times a day he got down on his knees and prayed, giving thanks to his God" in full view of everyone (6:10). Knowing Daniel's commitment to maintain this regular practice, his enemies used it as a basis to set up a scheme that would not only bring Daniel down but lead to his execution.

Note that these evil leaders had absolutely no question regarding what Daniel would do in spite of the proposal they were about to make to the king. Though his life would be in danger, they were convinced that Daniel would not waver in his prayer practice. This demonstrates that they also knew much about Daniel's religious background and his character. He had *never* been unfaithful to or ashamed of his God.

These men also knew a lot about King Darius. Though he was a brilliant leader, like most men in this kind of position, he had a huge ego. But for Darius, this was a serious weakness—in this case, a noticeable blind spot! Combining Daniel's commitment to daily prayer with Darius's tendency to make naive decisions when his ego was involved, they developed an insidious strategy. Their speech before the king speaks for itself:

> "O King Darius, live forever! The royal administrators, prefects, satraps, advisers and governors have all agreed that the king should issue an edict and enforce the decree that anyone who prays to any god or man during the next thirty days, except to you, O king, shall be thrown into the lions' den. Now, O king, issue a decree and put it in writing so that it cannot be altered—in accordance with the laws of the Medes and Persians, which cannot be repealed" (6:6–8).

What a way to appeal to the king's ego! They informed him that *everyone* had agreed to this proposal. They even detailed in dramatic fashion who these people were. How could he refuse all of these loyal subjects who wanted to pay such a great tribute to him?

Furthermore, this plan made the king equal with their pagan deities. For thirty days, no one could even pray to a god or to any other man without suffering dire consequences—death in a den of lions. Again, what adoration!

Finally, they told the king they wanted to make his proposal public—to put it in writing—demonstrating to everyone how great and powerful the king actually was. To make this decree an unchangeable law would only exalt Darius even more.

There were also some subtle and deceitful recommendations in this proposal that were deliberately designed to cloud Darius's mind and influence his decision. If so many agreed, then why worry about anyone violating the law? After all, they reported that the "royal administrators" agreed to this plan, which would also include Daniel. Why not make such a decree? He could only benefit and at the same time, not hurt anyone. Furthermore, it was only for thirty days! Certainly no one would take a chance on violating this decree and suffering the consequences during such a short period of time. Right? Wrong! Daniel continued to pray three times a day, just as his enemies knew he would. It was an ingenious though insidious plot—and it worked just as they had planned.

## Daniel's Faithful Witness (6:10)

Daniel was obviously not aware of this conspiracy against him until the king issued the decree. But from the moment he found out, he never wavered in his convictions. Probably hearing about it while he was in his office, "he went home to his upstairs room where the windows opened towards Jerusalem." There "he got down on his knees and prayed, giving thanks to his God, just as he had done before" (6:10).

This is the kind of spiritual conviction Daniel had the first time we met him at age fifteen. When he was brought as a captive to Babylon and faced the fact that he had to eat food that violated Jewish laws and more specifically would convey to others an alignment with false gods, he "resolved not to defile himself with the royal food and wine" (1:8). Now decades later, could he do less as an old man who had never violated his spiritual convictions?

Knowing the consequences of these actions, how easy it would have been for Daniel to rationalize! After all, he *had* been faithful for all these years. Why be concerned about one month? Furthermore, why pray in public since God hears us in private as well? Certainly God would understand. And why interfere with God's plan to allow him to serve in such a key position in the Persian empire?

Personally, I don't believe Daniel wavered for one moment. If he did, it would have been a passing thought. This old prophet had a principle within his soul that guided everything he did.

There is one significant difference between Daniel's original stand for holiness as a fifteen-year old and his decision to continue his prayer routine at age eighty-three. In the first instance, he asked permission from the chief official who was assigned to watch over him (1:8). In this second instance, he did not appeal to anyone. Though he certainly could have had an audience with the king and explained what these men were doing, he did not.

Did Daniel know in his heart that God would shut the lions' mouths? I don't think so. What he did know was that God *could* save him. Like his three friends who faced the fiery furnace years before, he was in essence "saying" what they had said:

> *If we are thrown into the blazing furnace [or in this instance, the lion's den], the God we serve is able to save us from it, and he will rescue us from your hand, O king. But even if he does not, we want you to know, O king, that we will not serve your gods or worship the image of gold you have set up (3:17–18).*

## The King's Dilemma (6:11–15)

Daniel's enemies were watching and waiting to report Daniel's behavior to the king. They knew it would happen quickly. And when it did, they first reminded Darius of his decree, and the king in turn affirmed his decision. With glee, they then reported what Daniel had done.

Instantly, Darius understood his mistake and serious error in judgment. His "blind spot" suddenly became his point of perception. He knew he had been set up and duped! Why hadn't he asked these men if Daniel had agreed to this proposal? Better yet, since he had such respect for Daniel, why hadn't he consulted him before he issued this disastrous decree?

When pride is blended with our "blind spots," we become terribly vulnerable and can quickly lose perspective. It's easy to act on our own initiative. In moments like these, our brilliance has little to do with our judgments.

The king knew immediately he had made a stupid decision, and he tried to correct it. We read that "he was determined to rescue Daniel and made every effort until sundown to save him" (6:14). No doubt he tried to negotiate with his other two administrators, but to no avail. They only rallied more support and went as a group, reminding the king "that according to the law of the Medes and Persians no decree or edict the king issues can be changed" (6:15).

Darius definitely had his back against the wall. For one thing, what would happen when Cyrus, the king of all Persia, got word of what his subordinate king had done? After all, Cyrus had already befriended the Jews by encouraging them to return to Jerusalem. He had even issued a proclamation honoring "the Lord, the God of heaven" and made it clear that Israel's God had "appointed" him to rebuild a temple in Jerusalem (Ezra 1:1–11).

In addition, if Darius changed his decree, he would be putting himself in a position of taking the law into his own hands. He had made a serious mistake in threatening the life of a prominent Jew whom he had made ruler of all of the former Babylonian empire, but he was now trying to change the rules—something that was never done throughout the Medo-Persian empire.

And one more thing: What would Cyrus think when he discovered that this whole issue revolved around a decree that honored Darius—a decree he had made placing himself even above any god? Indeed, Darius faced a serious dilemma. Not only did he face the prospect of horrible public humiliation, but he could also be deposed, if not beheaded! He, too, was a man under authority.

## *The King's Decision (6:16–24)*

With no way out, Darius accepted reality. He issued the order to put Daniel in the den of lions. However, he did so hoping that Daniel's God would save him. This demonstrates his deep respect for both Daniel and his God.

The king then returned to his palace, unable to sleep all night long. He even denied himself any form of entertainment that evening and refused to eat. At the crack of dawn, he got up from his bed where he had spent the night tossing and turning and hurriedly made his way to the lions' den. With anguish in his voice and hoping against hope, he called out to his trusted administrator, the man he had assigned to oversee his whole kingdom: "'Daniel, servant of the living God, has your God, whom you serve continually, been able to rescue you from the lions?'" (6:20).

Imagine the king's elated response when he heard Daniel's voice! The facts are he "was overjoyed" (6:23). He then issued an order that Daniel be removed from the pit and that all those who had falsely accused him be thrown in the den—along with their wives and children (6:24)! How sad that innocent people suffer because of wicked and hard hearts.

But also, what irony! These men suffered the fate they had so cunningly designed for Daniel.

## A New Decree (6:25–28)

Following this dramatic event, Darius issued a new order that stood out in stark contrast to his first one. In his first decree, he honored himself, actually setting himself up as a god. In this decree, he honored the one true God:

> *"For he is the living God*
> *and he endures forever;*
> *his kingdom will not be destroyed,*
> *his dominion will never end.*
> *He rescues and he saves;*
> *he performs signs and wonders*
> *in the heavens and on the earth.*
> *He has rescued Daniel*
> *from the power of the lions" (6:26–27).*

We are not told how long Daniel lived following this great spiritual victory. However, we do know that he "prospered during the reign of Darius and the reign of Cyrus the Persian" (6:28). He continued to be a witness for the God he served and a man the Lord used to help deliver His people from bondage. Daniel continued to serve as a mouthpiece for God—one of the greatest prophets who ever lived. As we'll see in subsequent chapters, his prophetic declarations form the outline for all human history.

## Becoming God's Man Today

*Principles to Live By*

*Principle 1. As Christians, we must always serve our employers (Christian and non-Christian) as if we're*

> *serving the Lord—giving our very best with our*
> *talents, abilities, and the gifts God has given us.*

This principle captures the story of Daniel's life. For seventy years he served pagan kings and never violated their trust. He was always diligent in carrying out his responsibilities—as if he were serving God Himself!

Daniel also illustrates a New Testament exhortation. Writing to the Colossian Christians, some of whom were still slaves, Paul wrote:

> *Slaves, obey your earthly masters in everything; and do it, not only when their eye is on you and to win their favor, but with sincerity of heart and reverence for the Lord. Whatever you do, work at it with all your heart, as working for the Lord, not for men, since you know that you will receive an inheritance from the Lord as a reward. It is the Lord Christ you are serving (Col. 3:22–24).*

Fortunately, few of us living today are slaves. This evil has been outlawed in our own country—thanks to a president who laid his own life on the line for his convictions. But this New Testament exhortation applies to all of us who serve as employees in various jobs. We are to carry out our tasks, not just to earn a paycheck, but to help our employers succeed. We too are to serve them as if we are actually serving Jesus Christ.

Peter underscored this same principle. He exhorted slaves to submit themselves to their "masters with all respect, not only to those who are good and considerate, but also to those who are harsh" (1 Pet. 2:18). Fortunately, in our own free society, we do not have to tolerate mistreatment and unfair business practices: we have ways to appeal harassment, or we can change jobs. But when we choose these options, we must also do so reflecting the fruit of the Holy Spirit. Even in our straightforward appeals, we have opportunities to be a witness for Jesus Christ.

I have a good Christian friend who faced a very serious problem in business. In actuality, he was cheated out of millions of dollars because of false statements and outright thievery.

He had no choice but to launch a lawsuit since he could not get any positive response dealing with the situation himself. However, even in this process, his attorneys were absolutely amazed at his Christian attitudes, his integrity, and his love even for his enemies. It was beyond their comprehension. It is possible, even in our culture, to follow the procedures outlined in the laws of our country and to do so in a Christlike way.

*Principle 2. As Christians, we must never hesitate or be ashamed to practice our Christian faith in front of unbelievers, understanding that we must do so with wisdom, discretion, and humility.*

Unfortunately, some Christians share their spiritual convictions in ways that violate the principles of Scriptures. Paul addressed this issue when he wrote to Timothy, instructing him how he should communicate with people who are hostile toward the gospel and the Christian way of life:

> *Don't have anything to do with foolish and stupid arguments, because you know they produce quarrels. And the Lord's servant must not quarrel; instead, he must be kind to everyone, able to teach, not resentful. Those who oppose him he must gently instruct, in the hope that God will grant them repentance leading them to a knowledge of the truth, and that they will come to their senses and escape from the trap of the devil, who has taken them captive to do his will (2 Tim. 2:23–26).*

I have a good friend, Mike Cornwall, who has served with me as a lay pastor at Fellowship Bible Church North for a number of years. He is also a banker. One Saturday morning, he and his wife, Sharon, were eating breakfast. As they looked out their kitchen window, a bus pulled up in front of their home. A number of people got off the bus, picked up signs, and began to picket in front of their house.

In a few minutes, a man knocked at the door with a document in his hands. He wanted Mike to sign a statement that his bank, a large savings and loan conglomerate throughout

Texas, demonstrated prejudicial decisions against minorities when making loans. Standing beside this man was another individual with a camera, ready to take a picture of Mike's reactions—assuming he would be angry—which would probably be displayed the next day in the *Dallas Morning News.*

In reality, what had happened was that the United States government had passed legislation that had been interpreted by minorities as prejudicial treatment. Since Mike was the CEO of this large savings and loan association, the minorities targeted him as a means to make their point. In fact, the leader of the group had actually come from another large city to organize this demonstration.

As a Christian, what would you have done in this situation? Frankly, my own reactions might have been less than mature. I do not like to be used in this way. But Mike's response was a beautiful illustration of what Paul was writing to Timothy and also illustrates how Daniel handled some of his challenges in pagan courts. Mike invited all of them into his home. Naturally, the man at the door with the document in his hands was totally surprised, as was the entire group. However, in a few minutes, they laid down their placards on the front lawn and marched into Mike's family room. Sharon served them coffee while Mike explained his personal concerns for minorities as well as the history of his own involvement with minority groups in the city of Dallas.

At a certain point in time, Mike shifted his focus from his involvement in social activities to an experience he had had several years before. Mike had come to know the Lord Jesus Christ as his personal Savior, which, he told the group, even intensified his concern for helping others. At that point, there was a decided change in the reactions of the group. He even began to get some affirmations from some of these strangers. Mike had won their hearts. They began to see more clearly his own perspective on what was happening in our society.

After a period of time together, the people stood up, thanked Mike and Sharon for their hospitality, and one by one walked out the door, got on the bus, and left—and were never heard from again.[2]

What Mike did in no way justifies what may have been inappropriately done by the U.S. government or any organization. But Mike took this opportunity to share his desire to be fair, honest, and nonprejudiced in his dealings with people—both in his personal life and in his business life. By practicing these principles in a nondefensive and open way, he was able to communicate the truth, not only about his own Christian behavior but the truth about Jesus Christ. And that's what Christianity is all about (John 14:6).

*Principle 3. As Christians, we must regularly spend time with God in His Word, in prayer, in praise, and in thanksgiving, realizing that we draw strength from the Lord to live a faithful Christian life as a result of this consistent spiritual discipline.*

This was one of Daniel's secrets in being able to practice the principles outlined in this chapter and in this total study of his life. He had prepared his heart daily to face these difficult situations. He had internalized God's Word. He knew when to take a stand and when to avoid conflict in an environment that was often very hostile to his own personal values.

There are lines, of course, we should not cross. This was certainly illustrated by Shadrach, Meshach, and Abednego. They could not bow down to an idol. Daniel concluded that to stop kneeling in prayer would be stepping over that line. But interestingly, it does not appear that these men had to take this kind of stand frequently, no doubt because they went about carrying out their assigned tasks with diligence and demonstrated wisdom and tact when they faced difficult situations.

Again, Paul spoke to this particular issue, this time in his letter to the Romans. Dealing with a Christian's relationship with pagan government officials, he wrote: "For rulers hold no terror for those who do right, but for those who do wrong. Do you want to be free from fear of the one in authority? Then do what is right and he will commend you" (Rom. 13:3).

There are exceptions, of course, as illustrated in Shadrach, Meshach, and Abednego's experience. But, generally speaking, faithful service in areas that do not violate our conscience helps us avoid situations that do.

## Personalizing These Principles

Please reflect on the answers to the following questions, which are designed to help you apply these principles in your own life:

1. To what extent are you serving your employer as if you are serving the Lord—giving the very best of your talents, abilities, and the gifts God has given you?

2. To what extent are you practicing your faith in front of your superiors, maintaining that intricate balance between not being ashamed of the gospel and at the same time sharing your faith in a wise, discreet, and humble way?

3. To what extent are you preparing your heart each day through prayer and reading the Scriptures in order to face the challenges you will encounter in your workplace?

*Set a Goal*

As you reflect on Daniel's experience and the principles we learn from his life, what one concern has the Holy Spirit brought to your attention where you need to make some changes? Set one particular goal and determine with God's help to carry it out immediately:

_____

_____

_____

_____

### Memorize the Following Scripture

*So whether you eat or drink or whatever you do, do it all for the glory of God. Do not cause anyone to stumble, whether Jews, Greeks or the church of God—even as I try to please everybody in every way. For I am not seeking my own good but the good of many, so that they may be saved.*
1 Corinthians 10:31–33

### Growing Together

1. What challenges have you faced in the workplace where it has been difficult to serve your employer as if you are serving the Lord? What challenges are you facing right now?

2. Have you faced any situations where you feel you have been fearful or perhaps even ashamed to practice your Christian faith in the workplace? On the other hand, can you share an experience when you may have been overbearing and insensitive? If so, what have you learned from these experiences?

3. Why is it difficult to spend time in the Word and in prayer in order to face life's challenges in the workplace? How are you overcoming these difficulties?

4. What can we pray for you personally?

# Chapter 9

# *Great Empires That Crumbled*
### Read Daniel 7:1–28; 8:1–27

*I* remember reading a report issued by two pastors who rather casually claimed to have had a vision—one that was similar to the apostle Paul's experience when he was "caught up to the third heaven" (2 Cor. 12:2). In fact, they used Paul's language and claimed to have received a special revelation from God.

I remember thinking at the time about Paul's report on this incredible experience when he wrote that the Lord gave him a "thorn" in his flesh to keep him from becoming "conceited because of these surpassing great revelations" he had received (12:7). We are not sure what this "thorn" was, but we know why God allowed it to happen. As godly and spiritual as Paul was, and regardless of his unique and special calling to be the great apostle to the Gentiles—a call that probably could only be matched in magnitude and significance by Abraham's call out of Ur of the Chaldeans—this supernatural experience could have led to pride and his downfall.

As I reflected further, I then asked myself the question—somewhat tongue in cheek—"I wonder what kind of 'thorn in the flesh' these two pastors received in order to keep them from becoming conceited and arrogant?"

My point is this. Today, some people claim to "walk in and out" of the presence of God and experience direct communication with Him as if it's like visiting the neighbor next door! Some even go so far as to claim to be special prophets whom God has chosen in these days to give us information that adds to the Holy Scriptures. Unfortunately, some claim to have had so-called "divine revelations" that even contradict the Word of God, such as predicting the dates when Jesus Christ will come again. They seem to have forgotten that Jesus Christ Himself stated that "no one knows about that day or hour" when this will happen (Matt. 24:36). Though God gave a rather specific timetable in terms of His first coming—which we'll look at in our next chapter—He did not give specific dates in terms of Christ's second coming.

## Troubling and Awesome Experiences

Receiving prophesies from God regarding the future were usually very traumatic experiences even for biblical authors. When the apostle John encountered the living Christ on the Isle of Patmos, he "fell at his feet as though dead" (Rev. 1:17). When Isaiah "saw the Lord seated on a throne, high and exalted," he cried out, "I am ruined! For I am a man of unclean lips . . . and my eyes have seen the King, the Lord Almighty" (Isa. 6:1, 5). And let's not forget that when Jesus Christ spoke directly to Paul on the road to Damascus, "he fell to the ground" and was struck blind and remained in that condition for three days. Paul was so overwhelmed with this experience that he couldn't eat or drink (Acts 9:3–9).

And so it was for Daniel. After receiving the first revelation recorded in chapter 7, he "was troubled in spirit" and "disturbed" (Dan. 7:15). But after the Lord explained the meaning of the dream—at least in part—he "was deeply troubled" and he was so overcome with awe that his blood literally drained from his face. He "turned pale" (7:28)!

Following the next vision recorded in chapter eight, Daniel had an even greater emotional and visceral response. He "was exhausted and lay ill for several days" (8:27). This old prophet was literally traumatized by what God had revealed to him regarding the future.

# *Holy Ground*

As we move from the historical section of the Book of Daniel (chapters 1–6) to the prophetic section (chapters 7–12), we are treading on holy ground. Like Moses' experience at the burning bush, we need to symbolically "remove our sandals" (Exod. 3:5). There is no basis for pride, which is sometimes reflected by Christians who claim to have unique insights into the future. Where Scripture speaks clearly, we can and must speak clearly. When Scripture is silent, we too must be silent—or at least tentative and cautious in communicating what we personally believe is God's timetable for days and years to come. As I personally approach this subject, I'm reminded of Peter's words when he was writing about the second coming of Jesus Christ: "But do not forget this one thing, dear friends: With the Lord a day is like a thousand years, and a thousand years are like a day" (2 Pet. 3:8).

Yet God definitely wants us to study prophecy. The Bible is a prophetic book. That's why the Lord inspired Daniel to record his dreams and visions. God wanted him—and us—to know, at least in outline form, what was and is going to happen in the future. This is also why He revealed future events to the apostle John which he recorded in the Book of Revelation and then inspired his servant to pen these words as a challenging preamble to this great apocalyptic piece of literature: "Blessed is the one who reads the words of this prophecy, and blessed are those who hear it and take to heart what is written in it, because the time is near" (Rev. 1:3).

# *Dreams and Visions (7:1; 8:1)*

What follows is not a detailed explanation of each verse in Daniel, chapters seven and eight. Rather, it's a "verbal and visual outline" that gives an overview of what Daniel recorded with a succinct explanation of the meaning of these visions in both chapters. As we'll see, much of what Daniel prophesied has already been fulfilled and can be verified in secular history. However, there are some major events that will definitely occur in the future. When this will happen, we do not know; but one thing is certain: Since many of the events Daniel prophesied have already happened, we can rest assured that the rest will take place in the future according to God's divine timetable.

We are not sure when Daniel actually recorded what we have in chapters seven and eight, but we can pinpoint the specific years when God spoke to him (see graphic on p. 3). The first dream and visions came during the "first year" when Belshazzar was appointed king of Babylon (7:1), and the second experience happened during "the third year" of his reign (8:1). Though Belshazzar did not officially recognize Daniel as an influential person in the kingdom as his grandfather Nebuchadnezzar had done, Daniel was still involved in some type of government service. Daniel himself made this clear in that after he recovered from the illness that resulted from the second vision, he recorded that he "got up and went about the king's business" (8:27).

Daniel was in his mid-sixties when he had these dreams. It would be another fifteen years before he was invited to Belshazzar's feast to interpret the handwriting on the wall (5:13) and several more years before he was sentenced to die in a den of lions. In other words, Daniel had these two different dreams nearly twenty years before he reached his mid-eighties, the time period when his life history is no longer recorded.

In Daniel's first dream, he evidently saw and heard far more than he recorded since he only "wrote down the substance of his dream" (7:1). However, he outlined some very specific details that are really not difficult to understand if we allow the Scriptures themselves to interpret the meaning of the symbols.

## A Half-Century Earlier (2:31–45)

Both Daniel's first and second dreams in chapters seven and eight are in many respects an extension of and elaboration on the dream Nebuchadnezzar had when Daniel was only fifteen years old and over fifty years earlier and that is described in chapter two (see fig. 4). This is the dream that Daniel not only interpreted but also recalled for the king. It involved "an enormous, dazzling statue" that was "awesome in appearance" (2:31). The head "was made of pure gold, its chest and arms of silver, its belly and thighs of bronze, its legs of iron, its feet partly of iron and partly of baked clay" (2:32–33). When Daniel interpreted this dream, he identified the "head of gold" as Nebuchadnezzar himself—and by implication, the Babylonian empire.

Daniel also explained that the other parts of the statue—in descending order—represented three additional powerful kingdoms that would arise and then crumble (2:39–40). Daniel then reported on a fifth kingdom that would be an eternal kingdom that would replace any previous empire. "This," Daniel wrote, "is the meaning of the vision of the rock cut out of a mountain, but not by human hands—a rock that broke the iron, the bronze, the clay, the silver and the gold to pieces" (2:45).

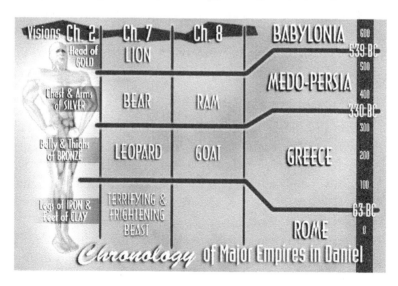

**Fig. 4 - Chronology of Major Empires Described in Daniel**

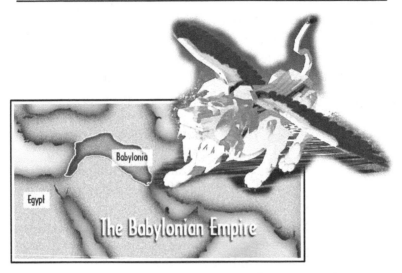

**Fig. 5 - The Lion–The First Beast in Daniel's Dream in Chapter 7
(This is also described as the head of gold in
Nebuchadnezzar's vision illustrated in Fig. 4.)**

## A Closer Look (7:2–7)

In Daniel's first dream, which is recorded in chapter seven, God changed the symbolism but it's clear that the four beasts that are described correlate with the parts of the huge statue that Nebuchadnezzar saw in his dream many years earlier. However, we have more specific details.

### The Babylonian Empire (2:36–38; 7:4)

The first beast Daniel saw "was like a lion, and it had the wings of an eagle" (7:4). Clearly, this beast represents Nebuchadnezzar and the Babylonian empire (see fig. 5). When his "wings were torn off," this event represents the time Nebuchadnezzar had a second dream involving an enormous tree that was cut down and stripped of its branches (4:10–14). Nebuchadnezzar was that huge tree. Because of his pride, he was stripped of his power, lost his mind, and lived like an animal for seven years (4:31–33). However, he was eventually restored to his kingship and acknowledged the one true God

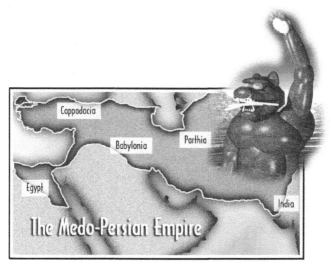

**Fig. 6 - The Bear–The Second Beast in Daniel's Dream in Chapter 7
(This is also described as a two-horned ram in
Nebuchadnezzar's vision illustrated in Fig. 4.)**

that should be honored and glorified (4:34–35). This restoration definitely correlates with the first beast in Daniel's dream when he "was lifted from the ground so that it stood on two feet like a man, and the heart of a man was given to it" (7:4). In other words, Nebuchadnezzar no longer lived like an animal but a human being.

## The Medo-Persian Empire (2:39a; 7:5; 8:3, 4, 20)

The second beast in Daniel's dream "looked like a bear" (7:5). This animal is aligned with the "chest and arms of silver" in Nebuchadnezzar's dream and represents Medo-Persia (see fig. 6). We know from secular history that Cyrus had three major conquests: Babylon (in 539 B.C.), Lydia (in 546 B.C.), and Egypt (in 525 B.C.). These conquests are no doubt symbolized by the "three ribs" in the bear's "mouth between its teeth" (7:5).

In Daniel's second dream, this second kingdom is illustrated with a two-horned ram (8:3) and is specifically identified in the biblical text as the "kings of Media and Persia" (8:20).

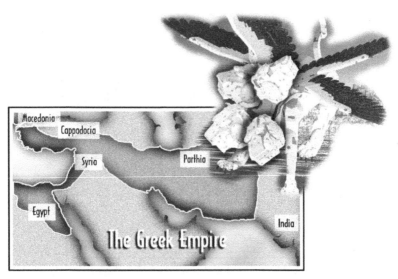

**Fig. 7 - The Leopard–The Third Beast in Daniel's Dream in Chapter 7
(This is also described as a goat in
Nebuchadnezzar's vision illustrated in Fig. 4.)**

## The Grecian Empire (2:39b; 7:6; 8:5–8, 21, 22)

The third beast in Daniel's first dream "looked like a leopard." It "had four wings like those of a bird." Furthermore, it "had four heads" (7:6). This beast correlates with the "belly and thighs of bronze" in the statue in Nebuchadnezzar's dream (2:32c) and is also aligned with the "goat with the prominent horn" that destroyed the "two-horned ram" in Daniel's second dream (8:5–7). Daniel identified this "leopard-looking" beast in his first dream and the "shaggy goat" in his second dream as "the king of Greece" (8:21).

Again, secular history throws a great deal of light on this symbolism. A leopard is known for his speed and thirst for blood. Alexander the Great conquered the entire Medo-Persian empire within ten short years (see fig. 7). This swiftness is also illustrated with the leopard's four wings (7:6) and by the way the flying goat in Daniel's second dream covered "the whole earth without touching the ground" (8:5).

**Fig. 8 - The Fourth Beast in Daniel's Dream in Chapter 7
(This is also described as the legs of iron and feet of clay
in Nebuchadnezzar's vision illustrated in Fig. 4.)**

Daniel also noted that the prominent horn on this goat was broken off and replaced with "four horns." In Scripture, "horns" represent power. Remember too that the leopard in the first dream had "four heads" (7:6b). History has clarified the meaning of this symbolism. When Alexander suddenly died from serious illness, the Grecian empire was divided into four separate entities ruled by four separate kings. Secular historians actually identify these men by name.[1]

## The Roman Empire (2:40–43; 7:7)

The fourth kingdom described in Daniel's dream is not identified with any living animal, past or present. However, Daniel described it as a good candidate for Jurassic Park. It was "terrifying and frightening and very powerful." This beast had "large iron teeth" that "crushed and devoured its victims." It then "trampled underfoot" anything that had not been previously devoured. This huge, ugly beast also had "ten horns" (7:7).

This fourth kingdom is definitely aligned with the "legs of iron" and the "feet partly of iron and partly of baked clay" in Nebuchadnezzar's dream (2:3). We can assume that the feet of the statue had ten toes which would correlate with the "ten horns" that Daniel saw on the beast in his first dream (7:7).

Though this empire is not identified in Scripture directly, most Bible scholars believe it represents the Roman Empire that crushed everyone and everything that got in its way (see fig. 8). It became the most powerful empire to date, destroying and absorbing every kingdom before it, particularly the Greeks. That's why secular history refers to the Greco-Roman Empire. The Greeks were intelligent and artistic people who were taken as influential slaves by the Roman armies.

## *The First Little Horn (7:8–27)*

Daniel was both intrigued and puzzled by the "ten horns" on this fourth beast. While he was thinking about it, another horn emerged—a "little one." However, it grew larger and stronger and eventually "uprooted" three of the other ten horns (7:8).

As Daniel continued to reflect on this unusual vision, he saw an amazing sight and recorded these words:

> *"As I looked,*
> *thrones were set in place,*
> > *and the Ancient of Days took his seat.*
> *His clothing was as white as snow;*
> > *the hair of his head was white like wool.*
> *His throne was flaming with fire,*
> > *and its wheels were all ablaze.*
> *A river of fire was flowing,*
> > *coming out from before him.*

*Thousands upon thousands attended him;*
　　*ten thousand times ten thousand stood before him.*
*The court was seated,*
　　*and the books were opened" (7:9–10).*

At this point, Daniel saw the fourth terrifying beast destroyed. In its place emerged "one like a son of man, coming with the clouds of heaven" (7:13). Listen to Daniel's words as he described what happened:

"*He approached the Ancient of Days and was led into his presence. He was given authority, glory and sovereign power; all peoples, nations and men of every language worshiped him. His dominion is an everlasting dominion that will not pass away and his kingdom is one that will never be destroyed" (7:13–14).*

Daniel didn't apprehend the meaning of what he was seeing in this vision. Consequently, he approached someone who was standing nearby—probably an angel—and asked for an interpretation. He was particularly confused by the fourth beast, "which was different from all the others" (7:19). He "also wanted to know about the ten horns on its head and about the other horn that came up, before which three of them fell—the horn that looked more imposing than the others and that had eyes and a mouth that spoke boastfully" (7:19–20).

## A Vivid Interpretation

The unidentified personage whom Daniel approached with these questions responded with an explanation that no one can misunderstand:

- *The fourth beast is a fourth kingdom that will appear on earth. It will be different from all the other kingdoms and will devour the whole earth, trampling it down and crushing it (7:23).*

- *The ten horns are ten kings who will come from this kingdom. After them another king will arise, different from the earlier ones; he will subdue three kings (7:24).*

- *He will speak against the Most High and oppress his saints and try to change the set times and the laws. The saints will be handed over to him for a time, times and half a time (7:25).*

- *But the court will sit, and his power will be taken away and completely destroyed forever (7:26).*

- *Then the sovereignty, power and greatness of the kingdoms under the whole heaven will be handed over to the saints, the people of the Most High. His kingdom will be an everlasting kingdom, and all rulers will worship and obey him (7:27).*

This explanation correlates very specifically with what happened in Nebuchadnezzar's dream fifty years earlier. Listen to Daniel's interpretation at that time regarding what happened to the fourth kingdom:

*"In the time of those kings, the God of heaven will set up a kingdom that will never be destroyed, nor will it be left to another people. It will crush all those kingdoms and bring them to an end, but it will itself endure forever. This is the meaning of the vision of the rock cut out of a mountain, not by human hands—a rock that broke the iron, the bronze, the clay, the silver and the gold to pieces" (2:44–45).*

The "little horn" that emerged in Daniel's first dream and uprooted three kings and then became a powerful ruler over this fourth empire (7:24) can be none other than the one described in Scripture as the anti-Christ (1 John 2:18). Paul named him "the man of lawlessness" (2 Thess. 2:3), and John identified him as the "beast" in the Book of Revelation (Rev. 13:1).

## The Revived Roman Empire

What does all of this mean? Since we know from history that the old Roman Empire eventually crumbled and disintegrated and disappeared—not because of a supernatural attack by God Himself, but through a process of natural moral and spiritual deterioration—how is Daniel's prophecy going to be fulfilled? There can be only one answer. The old Roman Empire will be restored, and this new configuration will be similar but yet different. There will indeed be "ten kings who will come from this kingdom." Among these kings, "another king will arise" and "he will subdue three kings" (Dan. 7:24). He will be energized by Satan himself.

Those who study prophecy regularly have carefully watched what is happening in this area of the world. This is why there was so much interest when the European Economic Community—usually called the Common Market—was organized. As a result of the Treaty of Rome (March 25, 1957), six nations formed a union—France, Belgium, West Germany, Luxembourg, Italy, and the Netherlands. Several years later, this union increased to nine members, adding Great Britain, Denmark, and Ireland. They actually worked out a common agricultural policy as well as other ways to work together. On January 1, 1981, Greece joined this union, bringing the number of countries to ten.

This development created a great deal of excitement. Was this the ten-king confederacy mentioned in Daniel's prophecy? A lot of speculation and enthusiasm was squelched, however, when Spain and Portugal became members, bringing the number to twelve.

The lesson is clear. We must be careful how we interpret events in history today. We can confidently say that much of what Daniel saw in his visions has come to pass. However, the ten-nation union—the revival of the old Roman Empire—is yet future. The "little horn" or anti-Christ has not yet emerged—at least not visibly. But all of this will happen in God's timing. And when it does, we can be certain that history is beginning to reach a grand culmination in preparation for the coming of the King of kings and Lord of lords to rule and reign.

## *The Second Little Horn (8:9–14; 23–25)*

There is another "little horn" described in Daniel's second vision. He too will emerge as an evil ruler and king. However, his man will not emerge out of a revived Roman Empire. Rather, he will emerge from the third kingdom—the Grecian Empire—and replace the four kings after Alexander the Great died (8:21–23).

Some people misinterpret this development as also a reference to the anti-Christ. However, this would create an inconsistency in the biblical record. The facts are, there is an event in history that correlates very specifically with what Daniel saw in the second dream. Most scholars agree that this second "little horn" represents the eighth ruler of the Seleucid Greek Empire, Antiochus IV Epiphanes, who reigned from 175–163 B.C. In our final chapter, we'll look at how this prophecy was fulfilled in 167 B.C. In many respects, he foreshadowed the "little horn" (the anti-Christ) in Daniel's first vision.

If most of what we have looked at in chapters seven and eight has already come to pass exactly as Daniel saw it in his visions, we can be sure that a day is coming when Jesus Christ will once again come to this earth and fulfill every jot and tittle that is described in this great prophetic section of the Bible—and in all of Scripture. This may happen sooner than we think, especially in view of the fact that the church of Jesus Christ will be removed from the earth before it happens. But that's another chapter in this exciting study.

## Becoming God's Man Today

*Principles to Live By*

*Principle 1. Since so many prophecies in Scripture have been fulfilled to the exact detail, we can rest assured that future prophecies will also be fulfilled.*

Dr. John Walvoord lists approximately 1,000 passages, some single verses, and some chapters, in his *Prophecy Knowledge Handbook*. Five hundred of these have already been fulfilled.[2] Please understand that these prophetic statements were written before they came to pass. Only those who deny the supernatural nature of these events attempt to demonstrate that they were written after they happened. When we eliminate the supernatural in the Bible, we destroy the very foundations of Christianity. We remove the primary reason prophecy is given: to alert us to God's overall plan for mankind from eternity to eternity.

Don't be led astray. God's time clock is set and running. Every prophecy in Scripture will be fulfilled. Just as the kingdoms described in Nebuchadnezzar's dream and Daniel's visions arose and fell, so "the court will sit," and the future world ruler called the anti-Christ will lose his power and "be completely destroyed forever" (Dan. 7:26). Then Christ's "kingdom will be an everlasting kingdom and all rulers will worship and obey him" (7:27).

Jesus Christ will come again, first to remove the church and then to rule and reign. The important question is, Are you ready?

*Principle 2. We must evaluate world history carefully against the backdrop of a very thorough knowledge of biblical history in order to avoid premature conclusions.*

The Lord wants us to be ready when He comes. However, we must be careful that we do not go beyond Scripture in interpreting what is happening in our present world. During the time I was writing this book on Daniel's life, a man appeared on the scene predicting the exact time of the second coming of Christ and actually named the man he believed was the anti-Christ. Unfortunately, some of the people in our own church bought into this man's false prophecies. Predictably and understandably, his predictive times have "come and gone"—without fulfillment.

This has happened again and again throughout history. Sadly, both Christians and non-Christians become disillusioned. Christian leaders will be held accountable for our overly enthusiastic approach in interpreting events in world history and correlating them with Scripture when, in fact, we are deceived. And if we are using "prophecy" as a means to manipulate people, we will be judged accordingly (James 3:1).

I recently met with several men who were involved in a "Christian cult." The founder and leader built a thriving religious group with very dedicated members, particularly in the area of financial commitment. In fact, this man superimposed on his followers the three-tithe system in the Old Testament, which generated an incredible amount of money from a relatively small group of followers. He then used millions of dollars to fly around the world in his corporate jet, supposedly talking with world leaders. In actuality, he was also indulging in the worst kinds of immorality and had done so for years. He used Bible prophecy as a primary means to manipulate and control people; and when his greed and immorality were exposed, he left thousands of people disillusioned. Unfortunately, this is not the first time this has happened in world history.

On the other hand, these cautions should not deter us from studying Bible prophecy and teaching these great sections of Scripture. However, we must constantly check our motives and the accuracy of our interpretations, particularly the way in which we correlate prophetic statements in Scripture with what is happening in the world today.

*Principle 3. We must also avoid trying to duplicate prophetic experiences in our own lives, and we must be very cautious in listening to others who claim prophetic knowledge that cannot be verified in Scripture, realizing that even in the biblical record God only chose a few select people to give us a view of the future.*

At this point, this principle stands on its own. However, it applies particularly to sincere people who seek to know the will of God and often attempt to simulate the experiences of Old Testament personalities like Abraham, Moses, Daniel, as well as Paul and the apostle John in the New Testament. We can easily become self-deceived. Without knowing it, we can become ego-involved and share these "experiences we've had with God" as a means to build up ourselves in the eyes of others.

Some people actually start out with very sincere motives, and then become sincerely deceived. In the process, they discover they can use this as a powerful tool to control people. This happens particularly to individuals who interpret Scripture in isolation from others and then rely on their own subjective experiences to verify what they believe they see in Scripture. This is why it's very important to always check our interpretations and conclusions with other mature members of the body of Jesus Christ. It's doubly important to be accountable when it comes to prophetic interpretations and applications.

*Principle 4. A proper study of prophecy will motivate Christians to lead more humble lives, to study the Scriptures more consistently, to worship and praise God more diligently, and to live more godly and Christlike lives.*

I began this chapter by citing a report that had been written by two pastors who claimed, like Paul, to have been caught up into the third heaven and received special revelations regarding the future. Their experience "with Jesus" was described in nonchalant fashion, as if it were something that happened every day.

How far removed from the way Old Testament and New Testament prophets related to these encounters with the living God! I do not question that the Lord can and does reveal Himself today. However, what we see and hear as people relate these experiences has a pseudo quality that falls far short of what we read in the Holy Scriptures. Furthermore, the people I've met who may have truly had these unique experiences are extremely cautious in the way they share them with others. Furthermore, they are very selective with whom they share these experiences. They are definitely marked by sincere humility.

Perhaps the greatest impact the study of prophecy should have in our lives is to lead us to live more holy and humble lives. This is definitely what Paul had in mind when he penned the following words:

> For the grace of God that brings salvation has appeared to all men. It teaches us to say "No" to ungodliness and worldly passions, and to live self-controlled, upright and godly lives in this present age, while we wait for the blessed hope—the glorious appearing of our great God and Savior, Jesus Christ, who gave himself for us to redeem us from all wickedness and to purify for himself a people that are his very own, eager to do what is good (Titus 2:11–14).

Peter expressed the same concern:

> Since everything will be destroyed in this way, what kind of people ought you to be? You ought to live holy and godly lives as you look forward to the day of God and speed its coming (2 Peter 3:11–12a).

## Personalizing These Principles

The following questions will help you apply these principles to your life:

1. How seriously do you take the prophecies in the Bible that Jesus Christ will come again?

2. To what extent do you understand Bible prophecy? How much time have you devoted, first of all, to studying the prophetic passages in Scripture and then trustworthy commentaries on these passages?

3. How cautious are you in evaluating reports of people who claim to have experiences with God that are similar to the experiences of men like Daniel and Paul? Can you evaluate these reports without being judgmental?

4. How is the great truth regarding the second coming of Jesus Christ impacting the way you live your life? What do you do from day to day that would be embarrassing for you if Jesus suddenly appeared?

## Set a Goal

As you reflect on these principles, ask the Holy Spirit to reveal the areas of your life that need special attention and then set up a specific goal:

_____

_____

_____

_____

## Memorize the Following Scripture

*So then, dear friends, since you are looking forward to this, make every effort to be found spotless, blameless and at peace with him.*
2 Peter 3:14

## Growing Together

1. Why must we approach the study of prophecy eagerly but cautiously?

2. What are some examples that you've become aware of in which Christian leaders have become overly speculative in attempting to interpret world events and how they relate to Bible prophecy?

3. How can we maintain balance in having an open relationship with God and being led by the Holy Spirit, and at the same time, avoiding the tendency to attempt to duplicate the experiences of Bible personalities whom God called in a special way to reveal His truth?

4. How have the great truths regarding the second coming of Christ impacted the way you live? How should they impact the way you live?

5. What can we pray for you specifically?

# Chapter 10

# *A Powerful Prophetic Perspective*
### Read Daniel 9:1–27

*T*he study of prophecy demonstrates again and again that the Bible is a supernatural book that has been inspired by God Himself. The whole of Scripture illustrates and verifies the validity of a statement made by the apostle Peter: "You must understand that no prophecy of Scripture came about by the prophet's own interpretation. For prophecy never had its origin in the will of man, but men spoke from God as they were carried along by the Holy Spirit" (2 Pet. 1:20–21).

In this chapter, we'll look at one of the most significant prophetic passages in the whole Bible: the "seventy-'sevens'" prophecy revealed to Daniel. We'll see a marvelous prophetic outline revealed to Daniel that can only be described as miraculous. Only a sovereign God could "make known the end from the beginning, from ancient times, what is still to come" (Isa. 46:10).

## *Astounding Reflections*

When Daniel received the "seventy-'sevens'" prophecy, the city of Babylon—the last fortress in the empire—had already fallen to the Medes and Persians. It happened just as God had revealed to Daniel in two visions—one in the first year of Belshazzar's reign and the second in his third year (7:1, 5; 8:1, 20). Belshazzar had been captured and killed in his own palace after Daniel had read and interpreted the handwriting on the wall (5:30). In turn, Darius had been appointed as king over the Babylonian area and subsequently discovered Daniel's talents and experience and elevated him to serve as one of his key administrators (6:1–2).

As an old sage and prophet, Daniel was very curious about what was happening. He certainly would have reflected back—probably many times—on what he had written as a result of his two visions approximately fifteen and thirteen years before. He was well aware that the first "great beast"—the lion representing Babylon (7:4, 17)—had fallen prey to the bear, which was the second great beast that "came up out of the sea" (7:2, 5). He also knew that this kingdom appeared as a "two-horned ram" in his second vision and that the angel Gabriel had specifically identified this animal as "the kings of Media and Persia" (8:20).

All of this had to be incredibly overwhelming for Daniel. He was seeing his own prophecies come true in living color. To learn more about these events that were unfolding before his very eyes, Daniel also consulted the writings of Jeremiah, a prophet who had been preaching in both Israel and Judah nearly seventy years before when Daniel was carried off to Babylon at age fifteen. Often called a "prophet of doom," Jeremiah had predicted Judah's captivity (Jer. 25:11), the very year Daniel and his three friends were carried off to Babylon (605 B.C.). But Jeremiah had also prophesied that this time of judgment would end. "When seventy years are completed for Babylon, I will come to you and fulfill my gracious promise to bring you back to this place," the Lord had told Jeremiah (29:10).

These words grabbed Daniel's attention. But even more so, Daniel was deeply moved by Jeremiah's reference to prayer:

> *"Then you will call upon me and come and pray to me, and I will listen to you. You will seek me and find me when you seek me with all your heart. I will be found by you," declares the Lord, "and will bring you back from captivity" (29:12–14).*

## A Model Prayer

Daniel took these prophetic words very seriously. This helps explain why he prayed with such intensity and perseverance. He knew the seventy-year period was almost over, but he also knew that God's deliverance would be based on fervent prayer. Consequently, he "turned to the Lord God and pleaded with him in prayer and petition, in fasting, and in sackcloth and ashes" (Dan. 9:3).

Daniel's humble spirit and attitude as he prayed demonstrates how seriously he took Jeremiah's words. But so does the content of his prayer. What he shared with God reflects sincerity and commitment to the Lord—characteristics that he had demonstrated in Babylon ever since he arrived on the scene at age fifteen. For nearly seventy years, he had maintained his spiritual equilibrium, never compromising his faith.

### Adoration (9:4a)

Daniel began his prayer by acknowledging who God really is: "the great and awesome God." In many respects, this sounds like a prayer Jesus taught His disciples to pray: "Our Father in heaven, hallowed be your name" (Matt. 6:9).

### Faith in God's Promises (9:4b)

Daniel next demonstrated his confidence in God's promises and in His unconditional love for His people. Consequently he prayed—"Oh Lord, the great and awesome God, who keeps his covenant of love with all who love him and obey his commands."

### Confession of Sin (9:5–16)

Daniel followed his statement of adoration and confidence in God with confession. "We have sinned and done wrong," he prayed.

This section in Daniel's prayer is the most elaborate—and rightly so. God's people had "been wicked" and had "rebelled." They had "turned away" from God's "commands and laws." They had "not listened" to God's "servants the prophets."

As Daniel continued this section of his prayer, he elaborated on why his people were in captivity. They had violated the Law of Moses and had experienced the "curses" that God said would come upon them (9:11–14; Deut. 28:15–68).

All the way through this prayer, Daniel included himself, particularly in the confession of sin. Four times he specifically said, "We have sinned" (Dan. 9:5, 8, 11, 15). Twice, he confessed, "We are covered with shame" (9:7–8). And with numerous other statements he also included himself:

- We have been wicked and have rebelled (9:5a).
- We have turned away from your commands and laws (9:5b).
- We have not listened to your servants the prophets (9:6a).
- We have not sought the favor of the Lord our God by turning from our sins and giving attention to your truth (9:13b).

When Daniel included himself in this confession, he was demonstrating true humility. Though Daniel fell short of God's glory as we all have (Rom. 3:23), he had lived a very upright life in Babylon and, as far as we know, never compromised his convictions. But he also knew he was one of God's chosen people. Consequently, he took personal responsibility for their corporate failure.

## Petition (Dan. 9:17–19)

Following Daniel's lengthy and detailed confession of sin, he made a specific request. Daniel's petition was for God's help and deliverance. The basis of his request was not their righteousness but because of the Lord's "great mercy" (9:18), as well as His own reputation: "'O Lord, listen! O Lord, forgive! O Lord, hear and act! For your sake, O my God, do not delay, because your city and your people bear your Name'" (9:19).

## An Angelic Appearance (9:20–23)

During Daniel's prayer, God sent the angel Gabriel to give him "insight and understanding" regarding His future plans for Israel (9:21; 8:16). Imagine this old prophet's emotional response when this heavenly messenger reported that as soon as Daniel had begun his prayer, God immediately responded with a special message, which the angel was about to deliver. But imagine even more so what Daniel must have sensed and felt when Gabriel told him that he was "highly esteemed" by the Lord. Though we know that God does not "show favoritism" regarding salvation—as Peter learned in his encounter with Cornelius (Acts 10:34)—the Lord does respond favorably to His children when they love and obey Him. This was certainly true of Daniel. What a thrill this must have been for this aged prophet, who had served God so faithfully all these years in this pagan culture.

## The "Seventy 'Sevens'" (9:24a)

The first part of this prophetic message involved a very specific time frame. Gabriel reported that "seventy 'sevens'" were decreed for the children of Israel and the holy city of Jerusalem (9:24).

### Israel's Past

The Hebrew word which Gabriel used was *shabua*, which literally means a "seven." Some translators use the word *week* which is confusing to the English reader, simply because when we use the word *week* we think in terms of "seven days." However, because Daniel was already "a man of wisdom and understanding," particularly regarding Israel's history, he

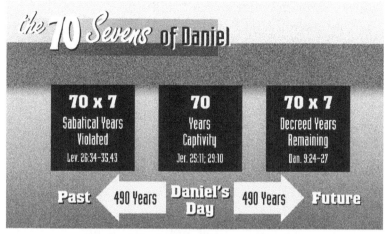

**Fig. 9 - A Backward and Forward Look at
God's Chronological Plans for Israel**

understood clearly that Gabriel was referring to "years," not "days." He certainly knew that according to the Levitical laws, they were free to use their land for six years and during the seventh year, they were to allow it to lie fallow (Lev. 25:3–5). He would naturally calculate that the seventy-year Babylonian captivity correlated with the 490-year period of time the children of Israel had failed to allow the land to rest on the seventh year (see fig. 9). Consequently, God removed them from the land for seventy years to make up for this disobedience. This is explained clearly in 2 Chronicles:

> *He carried into exile to Babylon the remnant, who escaped from the sword, and they became servants to him and his sons until the kingdom of Persia came to power. The land enjoyed its Sabbath rests; all the time of its desolation it rested, until the seventy years were completed in fulfillment of the word of the Lord spoken by Jeremiah (2 Chron. 36:20–21).*

## Israel's Future

The children of Israel had violated the Sabbath for 490 years—exactly "seventy 'sevens'" of years. This is fascinating since Gabriel now introduced Daniel specifically to another "seventy 'sevens'" (70 x 7 years) that were "decreed" for his "people" and his "holy city." With his understanding that "seven" was a significant time frame for Israel, he would understand immediately that Gabriel was referring to another 490 years yet future (see fig. 9).

## A Prophetic Message About Israel (9:24b)

Following Gabriel's reference to the seventy "sevens," he first made it very clear that the rest of the message he was about to deliver was for Daniel's own people (9:24a). This was not a prophecy about the Gentile world—as the previous visions portrayed (Babylon, Medo-Persia, Greece, and the Roman Empire—see figs. 4–8 in chap. 9). This message focused very specifically on the children of Israel.

Second, Gabriel stated that this prophecy related to Jerusalem. This was the "holy city" and had been ever since they had conquered the land of Canaan under Joshua's leadership. This was Daniel's place of residence before he was transported to Babylon (1:1–2). This is where the temple had been built to serve as a special place to worship God.

Third, Gabriel stated that when the seventy "sevens" (490 years) are complete, "sin" among the children of Israel will no longer be a problem. Transgression will be finished. And all past "wickedness" will have been atoned for (9:24c).

Gabriel reinforced these three interrelated negative elements that will be eliminated with three positive elements that will replace the negatives. First, there will be "everlasting righteousness" in Israel—the opposite of present and temporal sin. Second, vision and prophecy will be finished—sealed up. Finally, "the Most Holy" will be anointed, an obvious reference to the Messiah (9:24d).

These are strange words for those of us who have never seen the fulfillment of these prophecies. Sin is everywhere—not just among Jews—and right now we are studying prophecies that are yet to be fulfilled. They have not been "sealed up." It's true that Jesus Christ has died, risen again, and returned to heaven—but He has not been accepted and anointed as Israel's king. As a people, they still reject Him as their Messiah. Clearly, what Gabriel was stating and Daniel has recorded is yet future—for Daniel and for all of us. Keep this truth in mind as we proceed.

To sum up, here are all of the elements recorded by Daniel after receiving this prophetic revelation from the angel Gabriel:

*Seventy "sevens" [490 years] are decreed for*

> *1. your people [the Jews]*
> > *and*
> *2. your holy city [Jerusalem]*
> *3. to finish transgressions,*
> > *to put an end to sin,*
> > *to atone for wickedness,*
> *4. to bring in everlasting righteousness,*
> *5. to seal up vision and prophecy*
> > *and*
> *6. to anoint the most holy [the Messiah] (Dan. 9:24).*

## *Terminus a Quo: The Beginning Point (9:25a)*

When will this future 490 years begin? Gabriel answered this question in the next paragraph. "Know and understand this," he said to Daniel. "From the issuing of the decree to restore and rebuild Jerusalem . . ." (9:25a).

There is only one "decree" in the Old Testament that relates to the rebuilding of Jerusalem. There are other decrees, but they focus on rebuilding the temple. However, when Artaxerxes wrote a "letter to Asaph"—who was in charge of the king's forest near Jerusalem (Neh. 2:8)—it evidently included official orders to help build the holy city, not just the wall. Furthermore, we know exactly when this took place.

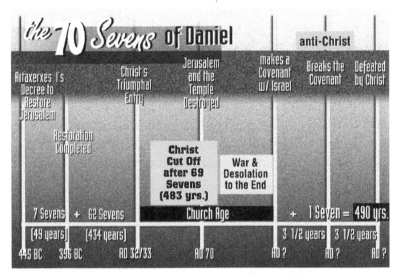

**Fig. 10 - Time Periods in Daniel's "Seventy-'Sevens'" Prophecy**

It happened in the "month of Nisan in the twentieth year of King Artaxerxes" (Neh. 2:1).

It is no accident that this is one of the most well-known dates in ancient history. The *Encyclopedia Britannica* reports that Artaxerxes became king in 465 B.C. His twentieth year would then be 445 B.C. Since all of this happened in the month Nisan, and since no date is given, we can assume that it was the first of the month. Consequently, a specific date in our calendar would be March 14, 445 B.C. If these calculations are anywhere accurate—and many Bible scholars believe they are—we have the exact beginning date of the "seventy 'sevens'"—that is, the 490-year period that Gabriel spoke about (see fig. 10).

## Terminus ad Quem: The Ending Point (9:25b–26a)

When will this 490 years (the "seventy 'sevens'") end? Gabriel doesn't answer this question immediately. Rather, he states that something very significant will happen at the end of

483 years. Specifically, we read that "there will be seven 'sevens'" (49 years) "and sixty-two 'sevens'" (434 years). Then "the Anointed One . . . the ruler" will come. Again, this can be none other than Jesus Christ, the Messiah. In other words, the Lord will make an unusual appearance after 483 years (49 + 434=483) or "seven 'sevens'" (49 years) plus "sixty two 'sevens'" (434 years). This unique event in the life of Israel that involves Jesus Christ's appearance will take place after the sixty-ninth "seven" ("seven 'sevens'" plus "sixty-two 'sevens'") and before the seventieth "seven" (see fig. 10).

Gabriel went on to state that Jerusalem would "be rebuilt . . . in times of trouble" (9:25b). This certainly came true under Nehemiah's leadership. The children of Israel were threatened on every side by their enemies, but they succeeded, finishing the wall in an incredible fifty-two days. However, the rebuilding process for the entire city was not finished until 396 B.C. in exactly "seven 'sevens'" or forty-nine years after Artaxerxes' decree (see again fig. 10). This is evidently why Gabriel mentioned the two time periods—"seven 'sevens'" (49 years) and "sixty-two 'sevens'" (434 years).

At this point, Gabriel made a great jump in time and elaborated on what will happen to Jesus Christ after the "seven 'sevens'" and "sixty-two 'sevens.'" "The Anointed One will be cut off and will have nothing" (Dan. 9:26).

What is Gabriel referring to specifically and when did it happen? To answer this question, we need to reduce the sixty-nine "sevens" to days. However, we must take one additional step before making this calculation. It is important to understand that a prophetic year in Scripture is 360 days, composed of twelve thirty-day months.

We are now ready for the calculation. Since sixty-nine "sevens" (or 483 years) would pass before the Messiah would be cut off, we can calculate the exact number of days—173,880 days. The calculation would be as follows: 69 x 7 years=483 years x 360 days=173,880 days.

What does this mean? The answer to this question is absolutely miraculous. God enabled Daniel to prophesy the precise time Jesus Christ, the Messiah, would be "cut off" (9:26). From the time Artaxerxes issued his decree to rebuild Jerusalem (March 14, 445 B.C.), this would bring us to April 6, A.D. 32. On this very day, the sixty-nine "sevens" would end and "the Anointed One" would come (see again fig. 10).

What actually happened on this day in New Testament history? Sir Robert Anderson studied this question very carefully and reported his findings in a book entitled *The Coming Prince.* Many Bible scholars acknowledge the validity of his findings. According to Anderson's painstaking calculations, Jesus Christ rode into Jerusalem on a donkey on April 6, A.D. 32 offering Himself to Israel as their king. This he concluded was the exact day Gabriel had in mind when he stated that "the Anointed One, the ruler" would come and then "be cut off" (Dan. 9:25–26).[1]

## *The Triumphal Entry (Luke 19:28–44)*

This is a classic passage in the Scripture. Jesus was headed for Jerusalem, the Holy City. He sent two disciples on ahead to find a colt. When they returned, they "threw their cloaks on the colt and put Jesus on it" (Luke 19:35). As they began to enter the city, a large crowd of the Lord's followers began "to praise God in loud voices," crying out: "Blessed is the king who comes in the name of the Lord!" "Peace in heaven and glory in the highest!" (19:38).

By this time, Jesus had been weeping over the city of Jerusalem. In the midst of His sobs, He said,

> *"If you, even you, had only known on this day [the day when the 'Anointed One was cut off'] what would bring you peace— but now it is hidden from your eyes. The days will come upon you when your enemies will build an embankment against you and encircle you and hem you in on every side. They will dash you to*

*the ground, you and the children within your walls. They will not leave one stone on another, because you did not recognize the time of God's coming to you" (19:42–44).*

## The Church Age (Ephesians 3:1–13)

Shortly after this dramatic event, Jesus Christ was crucified. He was totally rejected as King of Israel. However, this began a whole new era in history that is not mentioned in Gabriel's revelation to Daniel. There is a great gap between the sixty-nine "sevens" and the seventieth "seven." Paul called it the "mystery of Christ" that was revealed to him and other "holy apostles and prophets" (Eph. 3:5). He then spelled out clearly what this means: "This mystery is that through the gospel the Gentiles are heirs together with Israel, members together of one body, and sharers together in the promise in Christ Jesus" (3:6).

Here Paul was talking about the age of the church. Paul along with others was especially called to "make plain to everyone the administration of this mystery, which for ages past was kept hidden in God, who created all things." Paul continued his explanation to the Ephesian Christians:

> *His intent was that now through the church, the manifold wisdom of God should be made known to the rulers and authorities in the heavenly realms, according to his eternal purpose which he accomplished in Christ Jesus our Lord (3:9–11).*

## The "Seventieth 'Seven'" (9:26b–27)

Following this "gap" in world history, Gabriel—not understanding what would happen during the church age (1 Pet. 1:10–12)—continued to explain what would transpire to complete the "seventy 'sevens.'" A ruler would come who would destroy Jerusalem and the temple (9:26b). This can be none other than the anti-Christ (see fig. 10). This evil man will make a covenant with Israel, allowing them to worship God in the temple, for one "seven"—or seven years (9:27a). However, "in the middle of the 'seven'" (or in three and a half years), he will break his covenant, forbid worship, and desecrate the place of sacrifice in some incredible way (9:27b). This will continue (as we will see in our next chapter) for another three and a half years "when the seventieth 'seven' is complete." At this point, Jesus Christ will return and carry out what Gabriel said would happen at the end of the 490 years:

> "Seventy 'sevens' are decreed for your people and your holy city to finish transgression, to put an end to sin, to atone for wickedness, to bring an everlasting righteousness, to seal up vision and prophecy and to anoint the most holy" (Dan. 9:24).

Here we have a definite reference to the second coming of Christ when He comes to rule and to reign for a thousand years.

## Becoming God's Man Today

*Principles to Live By*

### Principle 1. God honors steadfast prayer that comes from a sincere, humble, and contrite heart.

Though Daniel had a unique relationship with God as a prophet, prayer is God's gift to every Christian as well as to the church. Together, we are to communicate with God on a regular basis. Consider the following exhortations from various New Testament letters:

- Be joyful in hope, patient in affliction, faithful in prayer (Rom. 12:12).

- And pray in the Spirit on all occasions with all kinds of prayers and requests (Eph. 6:18).

- Do not be anxious about anything, but in everything, by prayer and petition, with thanksgiving, present your requests to God (Phil. 4:6).

- Devote yourselves to prayer, being watchful and thankful (Col. 4:2).

I am convinced that God also honors the process that Daniel used in his prayers: first, adoration, second, faith in God's promises, third, confession of sin, and fourth, a specific petition.

Nehemiah took the same identical approach in his prayers when he received a dismal report about the Jewish remnant in Jerusalem. Those who had "survived the exile" and who were "back in the province" were "in great trouble and disgrace." The great wall surrounding Jerusalem was in a shambles and the gates had been destroyed by fire (Neh. 1:1–3).

Nehemiah was terribly distressed over this report. Like Daniel, he "sat down and wept" and "mourned and fasted" before he prayed (1:4). Furthermore, the content of his prayer follows the same sequence. His specific petition to have favor with King Artaxerxes (1:11) was preceded first with adoration (1:5a), then a statement of faith in God's promise to keep His covenant of love (1:5b) and third, personal and corporate confession of sin (1:6–8).

I have personally used this same process in leading the people in our church to pray about specific issues that definitely are beyond our reach. For example, in one church that was just starting, we needed a piece of property in order to build a building. However, in this particular section of the city, it was virtually impossible to find property, and what little was available was far beyond our reach financially. However, I led our people through this prayer process. We began by *honoring God* as "the great and awesome God." I remember vividly how we used the great hymn, "How Great Thou Art" as a means to voice our corporate exaltation.

Next, *we reminded God of His wonderful promises* to us. Again, I remember so clearly how people stood and shared with God the very Scriptures He had given us, reminding Him that we too believed He is a God who keeps His promises.

Next, several of our elders in the church led the whole congregation in a *prayer of confession*, acknowledging before God those sins that we had committed against the Lord, personally and corporately.

Our final step was to be very specific in our prayers, just as Daniel and Nehemiah were. We *petitioned the Lord for help in securing a piece of property.* We even followed Nehemiah's basic prayer and asked the Lord to give us favor with someone in this part of Dallas who could help us.

What amazed us all is that the person who could build a bridge to someone who could help us was sitting in the congregation for the first time. That person was so impressed with the prayer process and our desire to do the will of God that she indeed built that bridge to a person who opened the door even more to others who could help make this prayer a reality.[2]

*Principle 2. God wants all people on earth to have an accurate perspective regarding His plans—past, present, and future—that is based on objective, verifiable truth.*

For many years, men and women who have worshiped at the shrine of the scientific method have attempted to eliminate the supernatural. How can any intelligent human being believe that God simply spoke and created the universe? And how can anyone believe that God, in a moment of time, created Adam "from the dust of the ground and breathed into his nostrils a breath of life" and he "became a living being" (Gen. 2:7)? And Eve—well, it's a nice story—but who in his right mind really can believe that God created her from Adam's rib? And Bible prophecies? That is certainly impossible. No one can predict the future.

## The New Age Movement

Who would have "predicted" that people everywhere would move away from the age of reason into a metaphysical, postmodern mind-set where many people believe almost anything? Psychic readers have created a billion-dollar business. People by the millions who have been reared in an environment that has denied life after death now believe in reincarnation—an idea that had its birth in Eastern mysticism. Prominent personalities—from presidents' wives to movie stars—consult metaphysical counselors who claim they have supernatural abilities to predict the future.

On the other hand, never before have people in general so ignored the predicted messages of the Bible. This is ironic in view of the way hundreds of prophecies have been fulfilled to the exact detail. In some respects, this reflects our self-centered society since people today are far more interested in the immediate future and their own personal comforts rather than in God's plans for the future and how they affect their eternal destiny.

## The Truth Sets Us Free

The fact remains that God has spoken clearly in the Bible, outlining for us where history is going. Satan, of course, is alive and well, causing people to follow teachers who have no verifiable evidence for their ideas.

Consequently, we must not stop teaching the prophetic Scriptures. This is why God spoke so clearly to Daniel in visions and dreams, revealing information that correlates so accurately with secular history. Furthermore, the Bible is filled with prophesies that have already been fulfilled, demonstrating the trustworthiness of Scripture. Since people are so interested in the supernatural today, we must not fail to capture their hearts with the Word of God that can change their lives—not just in the here and now, but forever. It's the truth that sets people free (John 8:32).

*Principle 3. God wants us to understand where history is going, but He doesn't want us to be so obsessed with prophetic events that we get sidetracked from being about our Father's business here on earth.*

Being about our Father's business has two dimensions: building the kingdom of God and making sure we are diligent in meeting our daily needs for food, clothing, and the other necessities of life.

### Building God's Kingdom

In terms of building the kingdom, we are to carry out the Great Commission of our Lord Jesus Christ until He returns. However, we must not focus so much on His "returning" that we fail to do what we should to have an effective ministry in the here and now.

For example, there are some Christians who refuse to invest their money in a church building. They argue that Christ's return is near and this is a waste of God's money. Ironically, many of these same people don't hesitate to invest their money in a home—which demonstrates that they're rationalizing. However, for many it's a sincere rationalization.

Church buildings in today's world are very important in reaching people for Christ. Obviously, we can be overly extravagant, just as we can be overly extravagant in the clothes we wear, the cars we drive, and the homes we live in. A "place to meet" that is permanent and convenient is a very important factor in today's society in reaching people for Jesus Christ. Once these people become Christians, of course, we can then help them to establish their priorities in terms of their material possessions.

Furthermore, we do not know when Christ will return. It may be in the next moment or conceivably it could be 1,000 years from now. Remember, for most of his Christian life, the apostle Paul believed the Lord would return before he died. The Lord withheld this information from him and it wasn't until he wrote his second letter to Timothy that he knew that he would die a martyr's death before the Lord returned. And, of course, it's been nearly 2,000 years since Paul penned his wonderful letters regarding the imminent return of Jesus Christ.

As Christians, we must be about God's business here on earth as if we have lots of time to preach the gospel—utilizing every conceivable resource and potential. On the other hand, we must be ready for Christ's return at any moment. In fact, as we've already stated, this should be a part of our message when we preach the gospel of our Lord Jesus Christ.

## Meeting Our Daily Needs

The second dimension of being about our Father's business is the way we work to meet our needs and the needs of our families. Unfortunately, ever since the founding of the church on the day of Pentecost, Christians have become confused about this issue.

The Thessalonians were a classic example. When Paul and his fellow missionaries came to their city preaching the gospel, these people responded with unusual commitment and dedication to Christ. In fact, everywhere people were discussing the way in which these people had "turned to God from idols to serve the living and true God, and to wait for his Son from heaven" (1 Thess. 1:9–10). Unfortunately, some of the Christians in Thessalonica took the second coming of Christ so seriously that they became lazy and unconcerned about meeting their daily needs. Perhaps they were just so excited about the prospect of being delivered from their earthly circumstances that they were spending all of their time talking about it and not working to earn a living.

Whatever the cause, Paul had to admonish these Christians. First, he wrote, "Make it your ambition to lead a quiet life, to mind your own business and to work with your hands" (4:11). Evidently, some of these believers who had inappropriately interpreted the doctrine of the second coming of Christ were using their spare time—which they had a lot of—to get into trouble.

Second, Paul reminded them that he had already instructed them when he was with them to work and not to use their Christian experience as an excuse for laziness.

Third, Paul told them that lazy Christians who do not work to make an adequate living are bad examples to non-Christians, particularly when they take advantage of others. Paul exhorted them not to "be dependent upon anybody" (4:12).

Unfortunately, some of these Christians didn't respond to these strong exhortations, so Paul had to write a second letter and become even more direct. No one could miss his point when he wrote, "If a man will not work, he shall not eat" (2 Thess. 3:10). Taken out of context, these words may appear to be harsh and insensitive. However, these people needed "tough love." They were not responding whatsoever to Paul's gracious and repetitious exhortations to "be about the Father's business" here on earth—which definitely involves diligence in making a living. In fact, Paul became very direct when he wrote to Timothy with instructions on taking care of needy family members: "If anyone does not provide for his relatives, and especially for his immediate family, he has denied the faith and is worse than an unbeliever" (1 Tim. 5:8).

## Personalizing These Principles

1. To what extent are you blending consistent and steadfast prayer with human effort?

   Though God wants us to exercise our abilities and be responsible human beings, He also wants us to call upon Him regularly for help and assistance in all areas of our lives. It will make a difference!

2. To what extent are you basing your view of life—past, present, and future—on the Word of God?

Unfortunately, even some Christians who claim to believe the Bible are dabbling in New Age religions, not aware that many of these teachings totally violate the Word and will of God.

3. To what extent are you busy doing God's will while at the same time eagerly waiting for "the blessed hope—and the glorious appearing of our great God and Savior, Jesus Christ" (Titus 2:13)?

The Bible teaches we should work hard and be responsible Christians as if Jesus Christ may not come for a long time. However, we should also live our lives as if Jesus may come the very next moment—"in the twinkling of an eye" (1 Cor. 15:52). Paul demonstrated with his own life that this is possible.

## Set a Goal

As you reflect on these questions and the principles they represent, what has the Holy Spirit brought to your attention? Set one specific goal that will help you to become a more effective Christian:

_____

_____

_____

_____

## Memorize the Following Scripture

*Make it your ambition to lead a quiet life, to mind your own business and to work with your hands, just as we told you, so that your daily life may win the respect of outsiders and so that you will not be dependent on anybody.*
1 Thessalonians 4:11–12

*Growing Together*

1. Why is it so easy for Christians living in a relatively afflu-
   ent society to neglect the process of prayer? What sugges-
   tions do you have to help us refocus our priorities?

2. How can we as Christians avoid becoming sidetracked
   into a "subjective theology" that is out of harmony
   with the objective Word of God? Can you share some
   examples where you've seen this happen? What were
   the results?

3. How can we avoid becoming out of balance in terms of
   focusing on our citizenship in heaven, and at the same
   time, being responsible citizens on earth? How have you
   struggled with this tension? How have you resolved it?

4. What can we pray for you specifically?

# Chapter 11

# A Real "Star Wars" Saga
### Read Daniel 10:1–21

$A$s I reflected on Daniel's experience in the tenth chapter, I was reminded of a rather dramatic scene in the first *Star Wars* movie. Darth Vader had emerged as a powerful man in the galactic empire. He was dressed in black, with a headpiece that hid his face. His heavy breathing added to his wicked image— the personification of evil. He had sold his soul to the evil side of an impersonal power in the universe called "The Dark Side."

Opposite Vader was a man dressed in a simple brown robe and hood. His name was Obi Wan Kenobi—a man who had resisted evil and turned his will over to the side of good, the positive power simply called "The Force." Both Vader and Kenobi had supernatural powers: one to control others for selfish and wicked purposes, the other to free people to do good and contribute positively to humanity.

As the battle raged between those on the side of good and those on the side of evil, Vader and Kenobi met in a deadly duel in a gigantic space station commanded by Vader. As they faced each other, Darth told Obi he shouldn't have come because he was now Obi's Lord and Master. Obi responded by telling his archenemy that if he cut him down, he would come back stronger and more powerful than ever before.

As they faced each other with light sabers drawn, Obi Wan Kanobi glanced at his friends Luke Skywalker and Princess Leia—both comrades for doing good—as they were about to enter their spacecraft and escape. When Obi saw that they were safely on board, he lowered his guard and purposely allowed Vader to strike. Suddenly, Obi disappeared as his robe and light saber fell in a heap to the ground.

This *Star Wars* saga is pure fantasy and certainly doesn't square with biblical truth. However, it wrestles with some issues that theologians, philosophers, and religious leaders have recognized from the beginning of time. Both good and evil exist in the universe and conflict with each other. The story also reflects what most hope will always happen—that good will ultimately triumph over evil.

## A Frightening Experience (10:1–3)

Though there are incredible theological distortions in this space odyssey, there are also some elements that reflect reality regarding God's great plan for the ages. This is why I thought of this battle between Darth Vader and Obi Wan Kenobi when I read about Daniel's fourth vision.

When Daniel received this vision in the "third year of Cyrus, king of Persia," he was absolutely stunned. What he saw involved "a great war." And when he began to understand what was going to happen, he realized this was no "Star Wars" fantasy: the "message was true" (10:1).

When all is said and done, there is only one reliable source for evaluating what is true and untrue, what is good and what is evil, what is right and what is wrong, and what is a correct picture of those invisible realities that exist in the universe. It's God's eternal Word as revealed in the Bible. Societies that neglect or ignore this source as a guide for living are perpetuating confusion and are ultimately destined to collapse.

After receiving this vision and understanding that some terrible times lay ahead for his people, Daniel was so distraught that he went on a partial fast for three weeks. He was so overcome with grief that he probably didn't even bathe (10:2–3).

Why was Daniel so emotionally distraught? We must understand that he and his fellow Jews had been slaves for seventy years. Because of their sins, many had lost their lives. They were just ending this period of captivity and Daniel had been hopeful that all of his people would soon be delivered to return to their homeland. His previous visions projected a time when there would be an end of "transgression"—when "everlasting righteousness" would appear and there would be no more visions and prophecies (9:24).

He certainly was aware that good things had already begun to happen. Many of his people had already returned to Jerusalem to rebuild the city because of Cyrus's decree. Personally, Daniel had been promoted as the key administrator over the Babylonian area under Darius and had miraculously escaped the den of lions. Though he was probably too old to attempt the trip back to his home city, he was thrilled and excited that others could return. And now—another vision—a great war that affected all Israel! It was more than this old prophet could handle emotionally.

## *An Old Testament Theophany (10:4–9)*

At the end of Daniel's three weeks of mourning and fasting, he had another vision. Standing with several other men on the bank of the Tigris River, which flowed about twenty miles east of the city of Babylon, Daniel saw a man who was obviously a supernatural being. Daniel was terribly startled—so much so that he grew so weak that he couldn't stand on his feet. As blood drained from his face, he looked as if he had died. He then slipped into an unconscious state, lying face down on the river bank (10:9).

Bible scholars disagree as to who this man was. Most, however, agree that Daniel's description of what he saw is similar to John's experience when he saw the incarnate Son of God on the island of Patmos (Rev. 1:12–16). Listen to Daniel's description:

*"I looked up and there before me was a man dressed in linen, with a belt of the finest gold around his waist. His body was like chrysolite, his face like lightning, his eyes like flaming torches, his arms and legs like the gleam of burnished bronze, and his voice like the sound of a multitude"* (Dan. 10:5–6; compare with Rev. 1:12–16).

Personally, I believe Daniel saw an Old Testament manifestation of Jesus Christ, a supernatural experience theologians call a "theophany" (see also Ezek. 1:26–28). If this person had been an angel—such as Gabriel who had appeared to Daniel before (8:16; 9:21)—why wasn't Daniel overwhelmed on these previous occasions? The answer seems obvious! Daniel had now encountered God Himself—an Old Testament manifestation of Jesus Christ.

Daniel's experience was in some respects similar to Paul's encounter with the resurrected Christ on the road to Damascus. He saw a bright light from heaven, heard the Lord's voice, and was so overwhelmed that he fell to the ground. We read that "the men traveling with Saul stood there speechless; they heard the sound but did not see anyone" (Acts 9:7).

So it was with Daniel. The men who were with him on the Tigris riverbank did not see the vision, but they saw the results and sensed God's powerful and holy presence. Consequently, "such terror overwhelmed them that they fled and hid themselves," leaving Daniel alone (Dan. 10:7).

## A Galactic Battle (10:10–14)

At this point, another supernatural personality entered the scene. Many Bible students believe this second person was the angel Gabriel, who had been sent on another occasion to answer Daniel's prayer (9:20–23).[1] This heavenly messenger reached out and touched Daniel. Still trembling on his "hands and knees," Gabriel reassured this old prophet that everything was going to be all right. He lifted Daniel to his feet and told him he was still "highly esteemed" by God Himself (10:9).

Continuing to encourage Daniel not to be fearful, Gabriel reported that God had heard his prayer from the moment he had begun to fast and pray and to ask for understanding regarding the vision.

This was the same message Gabriel gave Daniel in a previous vision (9:23). However, this time this powerful angel reported that the "prince of the Persian kingdom" had restrained him for twenty-one days—which explains the three-week time period Daniel mourned. However, when Michael—another very powerful angel—came to help Gabriel, he was able to continue his journey through space and time in order to carry out his divine mission. "Now," he reported, "I have come to explain to you what will happen to your people in the future, for the vision concerns a time yet to come" (10:14).

## Satan's Restricted Domain (10:15–21)

This reference to the "prince of Persia" is one of the most interesting facets of this whole story. Who is this "prince" or "king"? Most believe that Gabriel encountered a powerful fallen angel—a demon—that Satan had assigned to influence the leaders of this great kingdom. Evidently, this evil personality was so strong that it took both the archangel Michael (Jude 9) and Gabriel to overcome his resistance (10:13). In many respects, this was a "Star Wars" battle—a fight between good and evil.

However, there was no impersonal, two-dimensional "force" involved in this conflict. Rather, this was a battle between the sovereign God, His emissaries, and Satan himself. Furthermore, even though Satan had incredible power, he was acting only within the parameters God gave him when sin entered the world. He could go so far and no farther! This is vividly illustrated in the story of Job (Job 1:12; 2:6).

As Daniel's story continues, he was still overwhelmed. These two divine encounters had left him "speechless" and physically drained (10:15). But once again, the angel ministered to Daniel. He touched his lips and Daniel was able to speak. Still expressing his anguish and his fear, he cried out, "My strength is gone and I can hardly breathe" (10:17). But Gabriel touched him again and renewed Daniel's strength, enabling him to listen to God's message (10:19).

Gabriel next informed this old prophet that he had to "return" to continue his battle "against the prince of Persia, and when I go," he continued, "the prince of Greece will come" (10:20). In other words, once the kings of the great Median and Persian empires (the "ram with two horns"—8:3, 20) are "trampled on" by the king of Greece (the "shaggy goat," 8:5, 21), Gabriel would have to do battle with the evil angel assigned to this new and even more powerful empire.

We can assume from Gabriel's message that Satan had no doubt appointed evil emissaries to influence every major empire that Daniel saw in his visions—Babylon, Medo-Persia, Greece, and Rome. Furthermore, we know that the greatest evil prince that ever lived will emerge out of the revived Roman Empire. In Scripture, he is called the anti-Christ. This man will not be an invisible and wicked angel. Some believe he will actually be an incarnate manifestation of Satan himself.

## The "Book of Truth" (10:21; 11:1–12, 13)

Before Michael returned to carry out his divine mission in the heavenly realms, he put Daniel at ease by sharing with him "what is written in the Book of Truth" (10:21). Figuratively speaking, Gabriel was referring to God's plan for Israel and the nations of the world. Chapters eleven and twelve in the book of Daniel unfold this plan in graphic detail. The first part of chapter eleven came to pass when Medo-Persia and

Greece emerged and then crumbled and collapsed (11:2–35). All that Gabriel shared correlates in every detail with what we read in secular history.

The rest of the prophecy is yet future and focuses primarily on the seventieth "seven" (the seven years) in the prophecy of the "seventy 'sevens'" that has not yet come to pass (11:36–12:13).

Toward the end of this experience, Daniel acknowledged that much of what he heard regarding the future of his people was still a mystery. "I heard," he said, "but I did not understand. So I asked, 'My lord, what will the outcome of all this be?'" (12:8).

At this point, Gabriel told Daniel that "'the words are closed up and sealed until the time of the end'" (12:9). In other words, Daniel had learned all that God wanted him to know. He could be assured that he had fulfilled his task nobly while on earth. He could depart this life in peace, being assured that some day he would be resurrected to receive a special inheritance in God's eternal kingdom (12:13).

## *The Mystery of the Church (Eph. 3:1–11)*

There was an even greater mystery that Daniel did not understand. He had no comprehension whatsoever regarding what would happen between the "sixty-nine sevens" and the "seventieth 'seven.'" In fact, no Old Testament prophet understood that there would be a gap of time that has to this present time lasted nearly 2,000 years. In fact, even Gabriel and Michael did not know what would happen. Even to this day "angels long to look into these things" (1 Pet. 1:12).

God designed this "gap" from eternity past, but, as we noted in our previous chapter, He only unveiled this mystery after the "Anointed One"—Jesus Christ—was "cut off" (9:26). It was a mystery "not made known to men in other generations" (Eph. 3:5a).

## Progressive Revelation

Even after Christ's resurrection, the apostles did not immediately understand this "gap" in God's eternal plan. This is why they asked Jesus just before He ascended back to heaven, "'Lord, are you at this time going to restore the kingdom to Israel?'" (Acts 1:6).

Jesus' response was specific and yet nebulous. "'It is not for you to know the times or dates the Father has set by his own authority,'" Jesus said. "'But you will receive power when the Holy Spirit comes on you; and you will be my witnesses in Jerusalem, and in all Judea and Samaria, and to the ends of the earth'" (1:7–8). The task was very specific. They were to preach the gospel to everyone. But the time frame between the beginning of the church age and God's continued plans for Israel as a nation were still hidden.

It took time for the apostles—who were all Jews—to understand God's plan for the church. Even Peter did not understand that Gentiles could be saved until his experience with Cornelius (Acts 10:1–48). Blinded by prejudice, he and the other apostles preached the gospel only to the Jews until God orchestrated this divine encounter in Caesarea. Interestingly, this happened at least five years after the church was born in Jerusalem. It was then that Peter stated:

> "I now realize how true it is that God does not show favoritism but accepts men from every nation who fear him and do what is right. You know the message God sent to the people of Israel, telling the good news of peace through Jesus Christ, who is Lord of all" (Acts 10:34–36).

## Paul's Unique Insights

Paul initially understood this "mystery" more clearly than any of the other New Testament apostles and prophets.

Writing to the Gentile Christians in Ephesus and throughout Asia, he made this point very clear. Note once again this passage of Scripture:

> *Surely you have heard about the administration of God's grace that was given to me for you, that is, the mystery made known to me by revelation, as I have already written briefly. In reading this, then, you will be able to understand my insight into the mystery of Christ, which was not made known to men in other generations as it has now been revealed by the Spirit to God's holy apostles and prophets. This mystery is that through the gospel the Gentiles are heirs together with Israel, members together of one body, and sharers together in the promise in Christ Jesus (Eph. 3:2–6).*

## Christ's First and Second Coming

Clearly Paul was writing about the "church" (3:10). It's only as we move into New Testament history that we understand what God had planned between the "sixty-nine 'sevens'" and the "seventieth 'seven'" in Daniel, chapter nine. Prior to God's revelation in Jesus Christ—involving His death, resurrection, ascension, the coming of the Holy Spirit, and the birth of the church—this was unknown even to Old Testament prophets. They saw clearly Christ's coming "to redeem" and "to reign," but they did not understand what would happen between what we now know are two separate events. Just as we can look at two mountain peaks in the distance that appear as one without seeing the valley between the two, so the Old Testament prophets could not see the great time distance between Christ's coming to die on the cross and His future coming to rule and reign (see fig. 11).

This can be illustrated with Isaiah's prophetic statement. First, he wrote: "For to us a child is born, to us a son is given" (9:6a).

**Fig. 11 - An Old Testament Perspective on
Christ's Coming to Redeem and Reign**

This is a prophecy regarding Christ's first coming to give His life on the cross, which, of course, has been fulfilled. But Isaiah continued without a break in his sentence, not understanding the church age: "And the government will be on his shoulders. And he will be called Wonderful Counselor, Mighty God, Everlasting Father, Prince of Peace" (9:6b).

This second prophecy predicts Christ's second coming to rule and to reign, which has not been fulfilled. Clearly, Isaiah did not understand the "time gap" between these two prophecies. So it was with all the Old Testament prophets, including Daniel. This was by divine design. It was a "mystery" yet to be revealed.

## The Rapture and Christ's Return to Earth

New Testament prophets also saw two unique events that they did not understand in every detail (see fig. 12). Paul particularly saw Christ's coming to remove the church from the world—often called the "rapture" (John 14:1–3; 1 Thess. 4:16–8; 1 Cor. 15:51–57). But along with the Old Testament prophets, New Testament writers also saw Christ coming to rule and reign and judge (Matt. 24:30–31; 2 Pet. 3:10) However, this introduces us to our final lesson in Daniel—the "seventieth

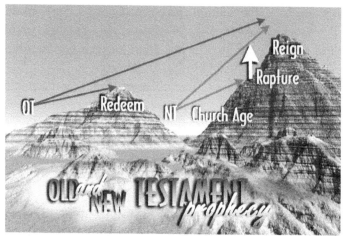

**Fig. 12 - A New Testament Perspective on Both the Rapture
of the Church and Christ's Coming to Reign**

'seven'"—often called the Tribulation period—and the rest of world history. Many believe that when the church is removed from the earth, this seven-year period will begin shortly thereafter and God will once again focus His attention on His promises to Israel. But more about this in our final chapter.

## Becoming God's Man Today

*Principles to Live By*

### Principle 1. Today God intends the church, the body of Christ, to be salt and light in our dark world.

As I read about the "prince of Persia" and the "prince of Greece," I couldn't help but wonder what evil "prince" has been assigned by Satan to influence the leaders of the United States—our recent presidents, the current Supreme Court and our Congress. Could this be why we have seen such incredible changes take place in the last decades? We have departed from our biblical moorings that directed the thinking of our founding fathers and kept Satan at bay. But we have changed the rules. As a result, we have seen a giant flood of evil permeate our society, resulting in abortion, pornography, foul and decadent language, murder, stealing, illicit drugs, rape, sexual abuse of children, premarital sexual activity, illegitimate births, divorce, etc.

Ironically, Larry Flynt, the publisher of *Hustler* magazine—a publication filled with sexual deviation of every kind—has in some circles become a national hero. While I was writing this chapter, Flynt came to Dallas to sign autographs in his new book detailing his sordid life. Even women, the objects of his lust and abuse in this magazine and book, added their blessings to what this man has done and continues to do![2]

Sadly, many people believe that Larry Flynt, Hugh Hefner, and their ilk, and their stand for freedom, is what has made America great rather than our previous commitments to the values embodied in the Ten Commandments. This is the ultimate in deception. But this should not surprise us in view of what Jesus said—even to religious leaders of His day:

> *"You belong to your father, the devil, and you want to carry out your father's desire. He was a murderer from the beginning, not holding to the truth, for there is no truth in him. When he lies, he speaks his native language, for he is a liar and the father of lies"* (John 8:44).

What is happening to our nation is nothing new in history. As we've seen, it has happened to the greatest empires of all time—Babylon, Medo-Persia, Greece, and Rome. They rose to power and then deteriorated and disintegrated. It should not surprise us that we see this happening to our own country—one of the greatest nations that has ever existed on planet earth.

But there is hope! This is why Jesus Christ left us on this earth as a church: to be light and salt in a dark world. We must remember that the darker the world becomes, the brighter our light can shine! The more people become confused and disillusioned, the more they will be open to the truth of the gospel.

*Principle 2. No matter how far we depart from God's will as a nation, as believers we have an eternal Presence who will never leave us or forsake us and who will help us live godly lives.*

God has not assigned an angel to watch over the church. Rather, He has taken on that responsibility in the person of the Holy Spirit. After Jesus returned to heaven, He sent "another counselor" to be with us "forever"—the "Spirit of truth" (John 14:16–17). If we allow Him to do so, He will empower us "to live self-controlled, upright and godly lives in this present age, while we wait for the blessed hope—the glorious appearing of our great God and Savior, Jesus Christ" (Titus 2:12–13). Furthermore, the Lord has provided us with spiritual armor with which we can defeat Satan. Listen to Paul's words to the Ephesian Christians, who lived in the midst of a decadent Roman Empire and in a city that was known for its demon worship:

> *Finally, be strong in the Lord and in his mighty power. Put on the full armor of God so that you can take your stand against the devil's schemes. For our struggle is not against flesh and blood, but against the rulers, against the authorities, against the powers of this dark world and against the spiritual forces of evil in the heavenly realms. Therefore put on the full armor of God, so that when the day of evil comes, you may be able to stand your ground, and after you have done everything, to stand (Eph. 6:10–13).*

We need not fall prey to the "Darth Vaders" in the universe! We have access to the true "Force"—not an impersonal, nebulous power or principle. We serve the Living God! He is a personal and eternal being—Father, Son, and Holy Spirit— three persons, one God!

Furthermore, Jesus Christ is no "Obi Wan Kanobi"—a fictitious figure who conquered the power of positive thinking and demonstrated the power of mind over matter, even in his own death. Rather, Jesus Christ is God, who became a man of history and, when He was "cut off" at the cross, came forth from the tomb as the resurrected Savior of the world! Though He is still "despised and rejected" by many (Isa. 53:3), He will one day assume His rightful place as ruler and judge. Then, "at the name of Jesus every knee" will "bow, in heaven and on earth and under the earth, and every tongue" will "confess that Jesus Christ is Lord, to the glory of God the Father" (Phil. 2:10–11).

In the meantime, we must always remember that we serve a God who "is able to do immeasurably more than all we ask or imagine, according to his power that is at work within us, to him be glory in the church and in Christ Jesus throughout all generations, for ever and ever! Amen" (Eph. 3:20–21).

## Personalizing These Principles

Following are some questions and observations to help you apply these principles, not only in your personal life but in all of your Christian relationships:

1. In view of the biblical reality regarding the body of Christ, what are you contributing to the strength of the church with your own lifestyle?

   No local church is stronger than the individuals, married couples, and families that comprise that body of believers.

2. Again, in view of this scriptural truth, to what extent is your own family unit a witness for Jesus Christ in the area where you live? What steps are you taking to

help your family unit become a beacon for Jesus Christ, reflecting the "true" light of the world?

If you are a parent, remember that in the New Testament, each family was the "church in miniature" and its maturity in Christ was measured by the degree of faith, hope, and love that it demonstrated in its neighborhood.

3. To what extent have you helped your family to put on "the full armor of God so that you can take your stand against the devil's schemes" (Eph. 6:11)?[3]

The charge to the Ephesians as a body of Christians was to put on the full armor of God. Though each of us is to put on this armor—which Paul describes as the "belt of truth," "the breastplate of righteousness," etc. (see Eph. 6:14–18)—this exhortation is to the whole church. Together, we are to put on this armor. The same applies to your marriage and to your whole family.

## Set a Goal

Using these questions to reflect on the principles in this chapter, what one goal do you need to set to be a more dedicated Christian? Ask the Holy Spirit to open your heart to at least one step you can take and then set a specific goal:

_____

_____

_____

## Memorize the Following Scripture

*For our struggle is not against flesh and blood, but against the rulers, against the authorities, against the powers of this dark world and against the spiritual forces of evil in the heavenly realms.*
Ephesians 6:12

*Growing Together*

1. In what ways have you seen the decadence in our larger society affect the spiritual health in your church?

2. What can you and I do to bring renewal to our churches to enable us "to say 'No' to ungodliness and worldly passions, and to live self-controlled, upright and godly lives in this present age, while we wait for the blessed hope—the glorious appearing of our great God and Savior, Jesus Christ" (Titus 2:12–13)?

3. How has the world's system—which the apostle John defines as "the cravings of sinful man, the lust of his eyes and the boasting of what he has and does" (1 John 2:16)—impacted your own life?

4. How has this same influence impacted your marriage and your family?

5. What can we pray for you specifically?

## Chapter 12

# An Unfolding Mystery
Read Daniel 11:2–12:13

When I was just an early teenager, I read two books that changed my life. Though fictional, their message was based on prophetic truth in the Bible. The first book was entitled *In the Twinkling of an Eye* and was based on Paul's letter to the Corinthians when he wrote:

> *Listen, I tell you a mystery: We will not all sleep, but we will all be changed—in a flash, in the twinkling of an eye, at the last trumpet. For the trumpet will sound, the dead will be raised imperishable, and we will be changed. For the perishable must clothe itself with the imperishable, and the mortal with immortality (1 Cor. 15:51–53).*

The second book was a sequel and was entitled *The Mark of the Beast*. This book told the story of what it would be like to be left behind following the great event described by Paul in this Corinthian passage, and to go through a period of history when an evil ruler will emerge who is identified as the "beast" in the book of Revelation (Rev. 13:1). Paul called him the "man of lawlessness" (2 Thess. 2:3). Under his leadership, no one will be able to transact business unless they have an identification number embedded in their skin. The apostle John wrote that "everyone, small and great, rich and poor, free and slave," will be forced "to receive a mark on his right hand or on his forehead, so that no one could buy or sell unless he had the mark, which is the name of the beast or the number of his name." We are then told that this "number is 666" (Rev. 13:16–18).

As I read these books, I was so impacted by the truth that was illustrated that I eventually became a Christian.[1] I say "eventually" because I resisted the Holy Spirit for a period of time as He tugged at my heart. In fact, if my parents had gone to bed before I returned home at night, I always cracked the bedroom door to make sure I had not been "left behind"! I remember kneeling at my bedside—as foolish as it now sounds—and asking Jesus to delay His return until I was ready. However, I could only fight this kind of conviction so long and soon knelt by my bedside with my mother and received the Lord Jesus Christ as my personal Savior. From that point forward, my fear of spending eternity separated from Christ and my loved ones was gone. I understood what Paul called "the blessed hope—the glorious appearing of our great God and Savior Jesus Christ" (Titus 2:13).

## The Fear of the Lord Leads to Life (Prov. 19:23)

Experiencing godly fear is nothing new in biblical history, particularly as it relates to prophecy. When Daniel first received the vision that he recorded in chapters 11 and 12, he was terribly frightened—so much so that he "mourned for three weeks" (10:2). He was especially concerned regarding "a great war" (actually many conflicts) that would affect his people. He knew that the "message was true," and it ignited great fear in his heart.

During this time of anguish, God reassured Daniel, first through a theophany—an Old Testament appearance of Jesus Christ (10:4–9)—and then through an angel, probably Gabriel (9:10–11). This messenger of God became the Lord's interpreter as to what this vision meant (8:16; 9:21). He also reassured Daniel once again that he was a man who was "highly esteemed" by God (9:23; 10:11, 19).

## *The Grecian Wars (11:2–35)*

Much of what Daniel saw in the future involved the Grecian Empire (11:2–35). What secular historians record regarding the "king of the south" and the "king of the north" is so detailed and in harmony with what Daniel recorded in Scripture that critics have concluded he must have written all of this after the fact. In their minds, Daniel couldn't have known these intricate details when he was recording future history. In fact, an atheist by the name of Porphyry theorized that the Book of Daniel was not written by Daniel at all but was a forgery written after all these predicted events took place—probably around 175 B.C.

Liberal scholars who reject prophetic phenomena in the first place were very impressed with this theory and promoted it—until a complete copy of Daniel was found among the Qumran Papers. This verifies that the Book of Daniel was written much earlier than Porphyry's theoretical date. In fact, scholars are in general agreement that because of these relatively recent archeological discoveries, Daniel must have written his manuscript during his lifetime.[2] There is only one logical conclusion: The Holy Spirit enabled Daniel in the waning years of his life to record exact details regarding the Grecian Wars long before they happened. In fact, Daniel did not live to see the fulfillment of these prophecies.

Unfortunately, people who don't believe that God uses His omniscience to reveal the future simply attempt to discover a way to explain away biblical prophecy. To do this, however, destroys the supernatural dimensions of the Bible, which in turn rips the heart and essence out of Christianity. This is why so many conclude that Jesus Christ was just another great moral teacher. Consistent with their presuppositions, they do not accept the fact that He was God who became a man.

## The "Illustrious One" or a "Mad Man"? (11:14–35) (The Second Little Horn—8:9–14; 23–25)

Antiochus IV was one of the most contemptible kings of Greece described in Daniel's vision. He named himself "Epiphanes," which means "the Illustrious One." However, those who knew his true character nicknamed him Epimanes—which means "the Mad Man."

This was not an exaggerated description of Antiochus Epiphanes. Perhaps this is what frightened Daniel the most. Because this evil king of the future would suffer several defeats, he would take out his frustration on the Jews. Antiochus would attack the whole Mosaic system of worship (11:28). Eventually, he would abolish the daily sacrifice and desecrate the temple (11:31). Furthermore, many of Daniel's fellow Jews would "fall by the sword or be burned or captured or plundered" (11:33). No wonder Daniel was frightened!

All of the events described in the opening section of chapter eleven (vv. 1–35) have come to pass just as Daniel saw it happening in this prophetic vision. Most notable is what is described as "the abomination that causes desolation" (11:31). We know from secular history that on December 16, 167 B.C. Antiochus constructed an altar to the Greek god Zeus just outside the temple on the altar constructed for burnt offerings to the eternal God. There he offered a pig to this pagan deity. Furthermore, he forced the Jews to also offer a pig each month to celebrate his own birthday. This was not only an "in your face" maneuver against the Jews, but also against God Himself.

## Jewish Heroes

Unfortunately, many Jews out of fear succumbed to demands placed upon them by Antiochus Epiphanes. However, there was a small remnant that revolted. Mattathias, a priest in

Israel who had five sons, stood his ground against Antiochus. He refused to engage in pagan worship. He and his sons escaped from Jerusalem, went into the mountains, and there began what has come to be known as the Maccabaean revolt.

The only reassuring aspect of all of this for Daniel was that this period of intense persecution would be relatively short. In late 164 B.C. and on into 163 B.C. , Judas Maccabeus—one of Mattathias' sons—restored and refurbished the temple. At that time, all the Jewish sacrifices were restored, and Judah once again had religious independence. Again prophecy was fulfilled. It was approximately three years from the time Antiochus desecrated the temple (Dec. 16, 167 B.C.) to the time that the temple was restored (in late 164 and early 163 B.C.).

## The Anti-Christ (11:36–45)
## (The First Little Horn—7:8–27)

What Daniel saw next in his vision has not come to pass—even to this very day. Here once again we encounter the missing seventieth "seven"—the seven years missing in Daniel's vision of the "seventy 'sevens'" (9:24–26). And here once again we meet the evil king described in two previous visions. He is the "little horn" that emerged out of the ten horns (the revived Roman Empire) (7:8). This is also the "ruler who will come" who is mentioned in the vision regarding the "seventy 'sevens'" (9:26). At that time, the Lord revealed what this evil man would do:

> "He will confirm a covenant with many for one 'seven' [seven years]. In the middle of the 'seven' [three and a half years] he will put an end to sacrifice and offering. And on the wing of the temple he will set up an abomination that causes desolation, until the end that is decreed is poured out on him" (9:27).

Though it appears that this may be Antiochus Epiphanes, this evil king is to emerge from the Roman Empire—not the

Grecian Empire—which is in harmony with what appears in the other visions in the Book of Daniel. And since Titus was a Roman, some conclude that all of this referred to him and his Roman army who leveled Jerusalem and the temple in A.D. 70. However, Titus never confirmed a covenant with Israel during a seven-year period. This can be none other than the anti-Christ—the evil and wicked man who is described in the rest of chapter eleven.

Note the unique activities of this king—which do not describe Antiochus or Titus or any previous king:

- "He will exalt and magnify himself above every god" (11:36a).
- He "will say unheard-of things against the God of gods" (11:36b).
- "He will show no regard for the gods of his fathers" (11:37a).

## What We Know That Daniel Didn't

Since Daniel's final vision, we now know much more than he ever knew. We know that the Greeks replaced the Medo-Persian Empire and that Rome eventually conquered Greece—just as Daniel prophesied it would happen. From carefully documented history, we also know that Jesus Christ came and that He was "cut off"—again, just as Daniel and many other Old Testament prophets saw in visions. We also know that Jesus Christ was miraculously resurrected after He died on the cross and was placed in Joseph's tomb. We have a documented record of His resurrection and His ascension, and we now understand what the apostles did not comprehend at that moment in history, namely, when the mystery of the church was unveiled it would be nearly 2,000 years before God restored the kingdom to Israel (Acts 1:6). This, of course, has not happened yet—but it could begin to happen before I finish this book on Daniel's life.

## The Rapture of the Church

As we noted in the previous chapter, Daniel never understood or even knew about the mystery of the church (Eph. 3:2–13). Consequently, he knew nothing of that unique event we call the "rapture."

Though this term is never used in the New Testament, it simply means to be "caught up" or removed from this earth. Paul also called this event a mystery in his letter to the Corinthians, the passage we looked at earlier in the opening paragraphs of this chapter. It will happen in the "twinkling of an eye" (1 Cor. 15:52).

Paul also described this event in his letter to the Thessalonians, explaining particularly what will happen at this moment to those who have died as true Christians and what will happen to those believers who are still alive when this takes place:

> *According to the Lord's own word, we tell you that we who are still alive, who are left till the coming of the Lord, will certainly not precede those who have fallen asleep. For the Lord himself will come down from heaven, with a loud command, with the voice of the archangel and with the trumpet call of God, and the dead in Christ will rise first. After that, we who are still alive and are left will be caught up together with them in the clouds to meet the Lord in the air. And so we will be with the Lord forever (1 Thess. 4:15–17).*

Jesus Himself gave His followers the first insight into this mystery. The apostles were deeply troubled regarding Jesus' statement that He was going to leave them (John 13:33). As their spokesman, Peter asked, "Lord, where are you going?" (13:36).

Seeing their anxiety, Jesus tried to comfort them with these words of hope:

*"Do not let your hearts be troubled. Trust in God; trust also in me. In my Father's house are many rooms; if it were not so, I would have told you. I am going there to prepare a place for you. And if I go and prepare a place for you, I will come back and take you to be with me that you also may be where I am"* *(John 14:1–3).*

What Jesus said at this moment is an entirely different message from His earlier statements regarding His coming to judge the world (Matt. 25:3–46; Mark 13:26; Luke 21:27; Rev. 1:7; 19:11–16). It's also a different message than the one often prophesied by the Old Testament prophets regarding the Messiah's coming to judge and reign and rule (Isa. 40:10; 59:19; Jer. 25:30–31; Joel 3:14–16; Hag. 2:20–22; Zech. 14:3, 4).

As we have already stated in previous chapters, the Old Testament prophets saw both the first and second coming of Christ, but did not see the "gap"—about two millennia to date—that existed between these two events (see again fig. 11, chap. 11, pg. 166). They had no concept of God's wonderful plan for the church where both Jew and Gentile would be one body in Christ. This too was a mystery that would be revealed in New Testament days.

## *The Seventieth "Seven" (9:27)*

When will the rapture take place? No one knows the exact time or date except God Himself. However, many Bible scholars believe that it will happen prior to the seven years or "the seventieth 'seven'" referred to by Daniel (9:27). Remember that Daniel was told that "seventy 'sevens'" (or 490 years) were decreed for his people—namely the Jews—and for the holy city of Jerusalem. However, at the end of the sixty-nine sevens (seven "sevens" and sixty nine "sevens" [483 years]), the "Anointed One was cut off" rather than recognized and honored as the King of Israel (9:26). However, following Christ's death, resurrection, and ascension, and the coming of the Holy Spirit, the mystery of the church was revealed to the "holy apostles and prophets" (Eph. 3:5). This introduced us to a period of time—the church age—that has lasted nearly 2,000 years. As far as we can tell, the seventieth "seven" has not yet begun.

## The Day of the Lord

When will this seven-year period begin? Paul also helps us answer this question in his letter to the Thessalonians. After answering their questions regarding what happens to those who die before Christ comes to remove the church, he went on to inform them that the "day of the Lord will come like a thief in the night" (1 Thess. 5:2).

Unfortunately, some think of the "day of the Lord" in terms of a twenty-four-hour day involving the rapture and/or the second coming of Christ to this earth. However, the "day of the Lord" begins after the church has been caught up to be with Christ. Furthermore, the "day of the Lord" lasts for centuries. It is not a moment in time. The "day of the Lord" is in contrast to the "day of grace" that was ushered in with the first coming of Christ. We have been living in this "day of grace" for nearly 2,000 years. By contrast, the "day of the Lord" will be characterized by God's judgment on this earth which will begin following the rapture of the church and last through the thousand-year (millennial) reign of Jesus Christ on earth.

## The Day of Wrath

Paul went on to reassure the Thessalonians that "God did not appoint (Christians) to suffer wrath but to receive salvation through our Lord Jesus Christ" (1 Thess. 5:9). In other words, God will not pour out His judgment on believers. This does not mean we will not suffer persecution and tribulation. This has happened to Christians throughout church history. However, the events recorded in the Book of Revelation involve tribulation because of God's wrath being poured out on people. This is a different kind of tribulation, which Paul said Christians would not experience.

Of course, the all-powerful God could protect believers from this wrath even though it is happening all around them. However, in view of everything we see in Scripture, it's more logical to conclude that Christians who are alive when the seven–year tribulation period begins will not be here because of the rapture.

## The Man of Lawlessness

Paul continued his reassurance to the Thessalonians in his second letter. Someone had evidently confused these new believers by convincing them that the "day of the Lord" had already come. "Don't let anyone deceive you," Paul wrote. "For that day will not come until the rebellion occurs and the man of lawlessness [the anti-Christ] is revealed." Paul then described what this evil person would do—which correlates with Daniel's prophecy regarding what would happen in "the middle of the seven" (Dan. 9:27).

This wicked king, Paul continued, "will oppose and will exalt himself over everything that is called God or is worshiped, so that he sets himself up in God's temple, proclaiming himself to be God" (2 Thess. 2:4). In other words, as Daniel prophesied, this man "will exalt and magnify himself above every god and will say unheard-of things against the God of gods" (Dan. 11:36).

Paul next pointed out that this lawless period of time would not begin until "the one who now holds it back . . . is taken out of the way" (2 Thess. 2:7). My personal belief is that this is a reference to the Holy Spirit, whose influence will be removed when the church—the body of Christ, in whom the Holy Spirit dwells in a special way—is removed from the earth. This will open the door for the anti-Christ to emerge and gain control—especially since he will be energized by Satan himself.

## The Book of Revelation

This leads us to another very important observation regarding the seventieth "seven" in Daniel's prophecy. This seven-year period provides a chronological structure for the period of judgment and wrath outlined in detail in Revelation 6:1 through 19:10. Furthermore, very specific time frames are given that correlate with Daniel's prophecy regarding the seventieth "seven" period. For example, note the following:

> They [the Gentiles] will trample on the Holy City [Jerusalem] for 42 months [three and one-half years]. And I will give power to my two witnesses, and they will prophesy for 1,260 days [three and one-half years] clothed in sackcloth (Rev. 11:2–3).

These are key verses in correlating Daniel's seventieth "seven" (the seven-year period) with these verses in the Book of Revelation. Since 42 months and 1,260 days (thirty-day months) are exactly three and one-half years, and since the anti-Christ "will put an end to sacrifice" exactly "in the middle of the 'seven'" (Dan. 9:27), this reference in both Revelation and Daniel must refer to the second half of this seven-year period. This is also what is no doubt meant by the angel's statement to Daniel that fulfillment will come after "a time, times and a half of time" (12:7).

We can assume then that the second half of the seventieth "seven" in Daniel is described in detail in the Book of Revelation, probably beginning in chapter six and ending with Revelation 19:11. Chapter six begins with the opening of the seven seals and 19:10 ends with the glorious coming of Jesus Christ to the earth to be finally anointed as "king of kings and lord of lords" (19:16)—a process that was interrupted when

He was "cut off" and rejected by His own people. As John states, "He came to that which was his own [his own people], but his own did not receive him. Yet to all who received him [both Jew and Gentile], to those who believed in his name, he gave the right to become children of God" (John 1:11–12).

## *The Big Picture*

There is a difference of opinion regarding when the church will be removed from the earth (see fig. 13). Will it be before the "seventieth 'seven'"? Will it be some time during this period of divine judgment on earth? Or will it be at the end of this period, making the rapture and the second coming a simultaneous event? Personally, I respect all of these positions; but I believe that all of the biblical data put together supports the view that the church will be raptured before the seven-year tribulation period or the "seventieth 'seven'" in Daniel's prophecy. The fact that every reference to the rapture is presented as an imminent event without any preceding time of trouble also supports this view. If this is accurate, figure 13 outlines what has happened and what will happen from Daniel's day until God creates a "new heaven" and a "new earth."

## Becoming God's Man Today

*Principles to Live By*

As we conclude this study on Daniel, I want to leave you with two very important principles. Both relate to one basic question: Are you ready to meet Jesus Christ, whether you live or die?

*Principle 1. Receiving the Lord Jesus Christ as personal Savior and experiencing forgiveness of sins is the only way to face eternity knowing that you will inherit eternal life and escape God's judgment.*

Jesus said, "I am the way and the truth and the life. No one comes to the Father except through me" (John 14:6).

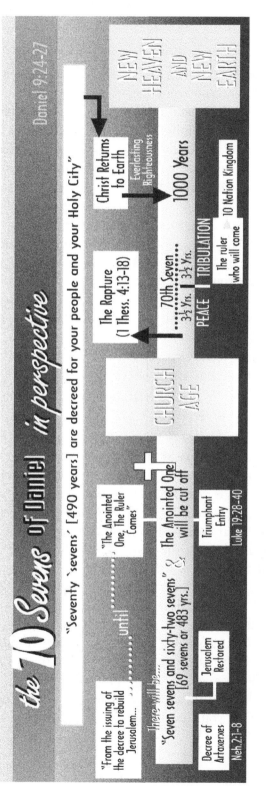

**Fig. 13 - The Big Picture—The Seventy "Sevens" of Daniel in Perspective (Daniel 9:24-27)**

All prophetic statements point to the fact that what Jesus said is true. There is no logical way to explain away this incredible claim. The Old Testament prophecies themselves and their fulfillment defy the law of probability. Furthermore, either Jesus was a liar or a lunatic—and to admit to either brings into serious question the ability of millions upon millions of people (including secular and religious scholars) to think rationally, clearly, and honestly.

As I shared at the beginning of this chapter, the Holy Spirit used the great prophetic truths regarding the rapture of the church and the judgment to follow to bring me to a salvation experience. To be frank, I was afraid of the possibility that I either would miss the rapture and be left behind or I would die before I was ready to meet my Maker. God used this fear to cause me to respond to the gospel. I'm glad He did.

Have you received the Lord Jesus Christ as your personal Savior? If Christ should come for the church or if you should die, are you sure you would spend eternity with God in heaven?

*Principle 2. As Christians, we should be ready at any moment to meet Jesus Christ face to face, either in death or if He should appear to take us home to heaven.*

As Christians, we should be motivated to apply this principle—not primarily by fear—but by love and a deep sense of gratitude for God's grace in our lives. Obviously, if we are deliberately and consistently walking out of God's will, we should fear God—just as children have a healthy fear of disobeying their earthly parents. We should also fear the discipline that God will ultimately bring into our lives when we deliberately walk out of His will (Heb. 12:7–11).

If you don't have this sense of fear and conviction when you deliberately sin, perhaps you don't really know the Lord Jesus Christ personally. Perhaps, as the Scriptures say, you're an "illegitimate" child (Heb. 11:3). To be specific, maybe you're not saved!

On the other hand, you may be saved and have simply hardened your heart. But this too should cause a deep sense of godly fear since you are in a very vulnerable position when this happens. Satan very quickly takes advantage of a seared conscience. When we lose our ability to decide between what is right and what is wrong, we're in a desperate situation—but never beyond redemption. The door to return to fellowship with God is always open.

## Motivated by Grace

But let's think positively and pro-actively. Once we truly understand God's love for us, there is no greater motivation to live godly lives for Jesus Christ than His grace. Paul captured this great truth in his letter to the Romans when he appealed to God's mercy as a basis for living godly lives:

> *Therefore, I urge you, brothers, in view of God's mercy, to offer your bodies as living sacrifices, holy and pleasing to God—this is your spiritual act of worship. Do not conform any longer to the pattern of this world, but be transformed by the renewing of your mind. Then you will be able to test and approve what God's will is—his good, pleasing and perfect will (Rom. 12:1, 2; Titus 2:11–14).*

As Christians, let's also remember that God has not called us to break fellowship with one another because of the various opinions as to when the rapture will take place. The important question that we all must face is, Am I ready? Can I say with the apostle Paul:

> *I eagerly expect and hope that I will in no way be ashamed, but will have sufficient courage so that now as always Christ will be exalted in my body, whether by life or by death. For to me, to live is Christ and to die is gain (Phil. 1:20–21).*

## The Doctrine of Imminency

Paul clearly taught that Jesus Christ could come to call Christians out of this world at any moment and that the "day of the Lord will come like a thief in the night." When he wrote the first letter to the Corinthians, he personally believed he would be alive when he was "changed—in a flash, in the twinkling of an eye" (1 Cor. 15:51–52). It appears that he did not know he would personally die before this incredible moment happened until he faced physical death in Rome. It was then Paul wrote his last letter. Writing to Timothy, he stated that the time had "come for my departure" and that he would become a Christian martyr at the hands of the wicked Roman Emperor Nero (2 Tim. 4:6–8).

But all through Paul's life as a Christian, he lived so as to be ready to be "caught up" at any moment. Paul's expectancy in itself demonstrates that there are no major signs or events yet future that will signal the rapture. Even the great apostle Paul, who had received wisdom directly from the Lord regarding this wonderful doctrine, did not know when it would happen. He too didn't comprehend the great span of church history we now know has transpired.

And so it is with us. Though we are certainly closer to the Lord's return than ever before, Peter's words written nearly two millennia ago are still relevant:

> But do not forget this one thing, dear friends: with the Lord a day is like a thousand years, and a thousand years are like a day. The Lord is not slow in keeping his promise, as some understand slowness. He is patient with you, not wanting anyone to perish, but everyone to come to repentance (2 Pet. 3:8–9).

Again, the most important question you must ask yourself is, Are you ready to meet Jesus Christ?

## Personalizing These Principles

- If you cannot answer with certainty that you know you would go to be with Christ should you die or should Christ return to take all true Christians home to heaven, you can be certain by sincerely taking the following steps:

Step 1: Humbly acknowledge to God that you are a sinner (Rom. 3:23). In other words, when our lives are measured against God's standard of perfection, we all fall short. Sincerely admit this to God.

Step 2: Believe that the Lord Jesus Christ died for your sins and the sins of the world. Be willing to repent and turn from your sins to follow Jesus Christ.

Step 3: Sincerely receive the Lord Jesus Christ as your personal Savior from sin. Invite Him to dwell in your life. Put your faith in His death and resurrection for salvation—not in any works that you have done (John 1:12; Eph. 2:8–9).

If you have sincerely taken these three steps, Jesus Christ now dwells in your life in the person of the Holy Spirit. You have been placed in His body, the church. Your citizenship is now in heaven. Not only has the Holy Spirit come to dwell within your soul, but He has also sealed your salvation until the day of redemption (Rom. 6:23; Eph. 1:13–14).

• If you are certain you are a Christian but you also know that you would be embarrassed and ashamed if you should suddenly die or if Christ should suddenly come, you can return to fellowship with Him this very moment and once again experience a close, abiding relationship. Simply acknowledge your sins and receive the ongoing forgiveness available in Christ's cleansing blood (1 John 1:9). As Paul wrote to the Ephesians, we must recognize our new position in Christ and "be made new in the attitude of" our "minds" and "put on the new self, created to be like God in true righteousness and holiness" (Eph. 4:23–24).

To understand this process more fully, read carefully Ephesians, chapters 4–6. Paul outlined clearly how we can "live a life worthy of the calling" we "have received" (4:1).

## Set a Goal

As you reflect on this study of Daniel's life and particularly these last two principles, what has the Holy Spirit impressed on your heart as your greatest need? Before setting a final goal, carefully review the goals you set throughout this study:

_____

_____

_____

_____

## Memorize the Following Scripture

*Be very careful, then, how you live—not as unwise but as wise, making the most of every opportunity, because the days are evil. Therefore do not be foolish, but understand what the Lord's will is.*
Ephesians 5:15–17

## Growing Together

1. What has been the greatest lesson you've learned from this study of Daniel's life?

2. Would you feel free to share the most significant change that has taken place in your life?

3. How has your view of Christ's imminent return affected the way you live your life from day to day? How do you want it to affect your life?

4. If you knew Christ was going to come within the next twenty-four hours, what two or three things would you want to do to get ready?

5. What can we pray for you specifically?

# Endnotes

## Chapter 1

1. Robert H. Bork, *Slouching Towards Gomorrah* (New York: Regan Books, 1996), 12.

## Chapter 2

1. David Casstevens, *The Dallas Morning News,* Monday, October 14, 1996, 18b.

## Chapter 3

1. Bill Nichols, "Keeping the Faith," *The Dallas Morning News,* Thursday, September 26, 1996.

## Chapter 4

1. The reference to Babylon no doubt refers to the city rather than to the "entire province" (see Dan. 2:48).

2. Dick Eastman, *The Hour That Changes the World* (Grand Rapids: Baker Book House, 1978), 13.

3. E. Stanley Jones, *The Secret of Effective Prayer* (Dallas: Word Books, 1967), 15.

## Chapter 5

1. Ray C. Petry, *A History of Christianity*, Vol. 1 (Grand Rapids: Baker Book House, 1962), 44–45.

2. "By Life or by Death" (words only), copyright 1938, by George S. Schuler; assigned to the Rodeheaver Company, 1959.

## Chapter 6

1. At this time, Saddam Hussein is rebuilding the city of Babylon. He actually portrays himself to his people as a modern Nebuchadnezzar.

## Chapter 7

1. Stephen R. Miller has made this helpful comment in interpreting why the term *father* is used here when it's obvious from history that Nebuchadnezzar was not Belshazzar's immediate father as we use the term in our language: "The term 'son' in Semitic language has a wide range of meanings. Wilson has listed seven ways in which the term 'father' was used in the time of Nebuchadnezzar and twelve possible meanings for 'son.' 'Father' may refer to one's immediate father, grandfather, ancestor, or as in the case of kings, a predecessor. Likewise 'son' may mean one's immediate offspring, grandson, descendant, or successor. Jesus was called the 'son of David' (e.g., Matt. 1:9–27, 12:23, 20:30–31, 21:9, etc.), although David was not Christ's immediate parent but an ancestor. Israelites called themselves 'sons of Jacob' (Mal. 3:6) and proudly proclaimed Abraham to be their 'father'

(John 8:53). Of course, the Jews meant they were descendants of Jacob and that Abraham was their ancestor." Steven R. Miller, *The New American Commentary*, Vol. 18 (Nashville: Broadman & Holman Publishers, 1994), 149.

2. The biblical text states that they used only the "gold goblets." Evidently, Belshazzar's servants concluded they didn't need the "silver goblets" to serve everyone as the king had ordered. In the Book of Ezra we understand why. The number of gold and silver articles totaled 5,400 (Ezra 1:11).

3. P. A. Beauliew, *The Reign of Nabonidus, King of Babylon 556–539 B.C.* (New Haven: Yale Varsity Press, 1989), 90, 156–157.

## Chapter 8

1. For a description of the secular sources for this information, see Leon Wood, *A Commentary on Daniel* (Grand Rapids: Zondervan Publishing House, 1973), 153–155.

2. See Gene A. Getz, *The Walk* (Nashville: Broadman & Holman Publishers, 1994), 201, 218–219.

## Chapter 9

1. Antipater, and later Cassander, gained control of Greece and Macedonia: Lysimachus ruled Thrace and a large part of Asia Minor: Seleucus I Nicator governed Syria, Babylon, and much of the Middle East (all of Asia except Asia Minor in Palestine), and Ptolemy I Soter controlled Egypt and Palestine. Stephen R. Miller, *New American Commentary*, Vol. 18 (Nashville: Broadman & Holman Publishers), 201.

2. Dr. John F. Walvoord, *Prophecy Knowledge Handbook* (Wheaton: Victor Books, 1990), 648–791.

*Chapter 10*

1. Though some calculations vary in terms of specific dates, the time frame is so close that it could not happen by chance. Many believe that Daniel definitely saw what we call the "triumphal entry" into Jerusalem by Jesus Christ. For a more detailed explanation regarding these basic time frames in Israel's history, see Alva J. McClain, *Daniel's Prophecy of the Seventy Weeks* (Grand Rapids: Zondervan Publishing House, 1969), 17–27; see also Harold W. Hoehner, *Chronological Aspects of the Life of Christ* (Grand Rapids: Zondervan Publishing House, 1977), 115–142.

2. For a more detailed development of Nehemiah's prayer process, see Gene A. Getz, *Nehemiah: Becoming a Disciplined Leader*, another book in the *Men of Character* series (Nashville: Broadman & Holman Publishers, 1995), 3–35.

*Chapter 11*

1. Though Gabriel is not mentioned by name in this passage, he is mentioned in Daniel's second vision (8:16) and in the revelation regarding the "seventy 'sevens'" (9:20–24). The person who "touched" Daniel in chapter ten (10:10) and interpreted Daniel's fourth vision played a very similar role to Gabriel. It makes sense contextually and functionally to conclude that "the one who looked like a man" in this chapter was the same angelic messenger. Consequently, Gabriel's name is used in describing what happened in this passage, even though it involves some speculation.

2. *Dallas Morning News*, Tuesday, January 21, 1997.

3. Note that Paul used the plural pronouns through-out this passage (Eph. 6:10–18), which indicates he was not just talking to "individual" Christians, but to a "group" of Christians. Paul intended that this military metaphor not only be applied to individuals but to all believers who are bound together in intimate relationships. This is what makes the church, the family, and marriages unique. As believers, we are in this battle together, and together we need to put on this armor in order to defeat Satan.

## Chapter 12

1. Both of these books are out of print. However, three current novels based on the same theme are *Left Behind*, *Tribulation Force*, and *Nicholae* written by Tim LaHaye and Jerry B. Jenkins and published by Tyndale House Publishers, Wheaton, Illinois (highly recommended reading).

2. John F. Walvoord, *The Prophecy Knowledge Handbook* (Dallas: Dallas Seminary Press, 1990), 263–264.